---   ---

REFILLING THE CHURCH'S FOUNTAIN OF YOUTH

---   ---

REFILLING THE CHURCH'S FOUNTAIN OF YOUTH

A Recipe for Emerging Adult Attraction & Retention

Nicholas A. Meade

Foreword by Lori D. Spears

Title: Refilling the Church's Fountain of Youth: A Recipe for Emerging Adult Attraction & Retention
Copyright © 2015 Nicholas A. Meade Ministries
Cover Model: Brielle R. Meade
Cover Art: His Visions a subsidiary of Inkspots Dzigns
Artist: Derek D. Lewis
www.visionsbyhim.com
www.isdpix.com

All rights reserved. No part of this publication may be reproduced, distributed, or transmitted in any form or by any means, including photocopying, recording, or other electronic or mechanical methods, without the prior written permission of the publisher, except in the case of brief quotations embodied in critical reviews and certain other noncommercial uses permitted by copyright law.

For permission requests, send an email to the publisher with the subject line "Copyright Permissions" to the following email address:

Nicholas A. Meade Ministries
publishing@nicholasmeade.com
www.nicholasmeade.com

ISBN 978-0-9861654-0-5

CONTENTS

Foreword		vi
Preface		viii
Acknowledgements		ix
Dedication		x
Introduction		1

CHAPTERS

Chapter One	Arriving At This Focus of Ministry	6
Chapter Two	Biblical Exemplars of Effective Ministry	17
Chapter Three	Perpetua's Emerging Adult Faith	49
Chapter Four	Lessons from Liberation Theology	72
Chapter Five	Expert Voices on Emerging Adulthood	89
Chapter Six	The Recipe Revealed	122
Chapter Seven	Looking Back and Looking Forward	168

APPENDIXES

Appendix A	Project Forms	175
Appendix B	Emerging Adult Model Ministry Survey	180
Appendix C	Interview Questions	185
Appendix D	Young Adult Activities Flyer	188
Appendix E	Data Collection Charts And Graphs	190

Bibliography 198

FOREWORD

When looking at the statistics of the traditional church enrollment, it is no surprise that the numbers are constantly decreasing. Additionally, it is no surprise that the largest population of decline is occurring amongst the young adults within the age range of 18-30. The two main factors that support the declining statics is the increasing population of the unchurched and the multiple streams of social media. According to the Barna Group, the number of unchurched individuals has almost doubled since 1991 and increased to approximately seventy-five million, many of which fall within the age range of 18-35. Further, the various mediums of social media eagerly provide exposure to services and churches through electronic means at any time, on any day with multiple options. Therefore, challenging the young adults who are constantly attached to the social media streams to disregard the need to enter into a physical building on a week-to-week basis to engage in worship.

The skillfully written research on retention and attraction of emerging adults, *Refilling the Church's Fountain of Youth*, is a strong testament to the rationale and reasoning behind the decline. In addition to rationale, the author offers a remedy to assist in attraction and retention within the young adult population. This work provides a pragmatic paradigm that challenges the reader to view the issue of retention and attraction from biblical, historical, theological and theoretical perspective. In the Great Commission, Jesus empowered the disciples to teach, compel, and baptize all nations. *Refilling the Church's Fountain of Youth* is a current day model, which serves as an educational tool while also demanding the reader to accept the challenge by identifying the problem and implementing strategies that will alleviate and or decrease the steady decline in emerging young adults within the church environment.

Nicholas Meade is a noted up and coming scholar and author who recently completed the Doctor of Ministry degree from United Theological Seminary in Dayton, OH. The book is a reflection of his research on retention and attraction of emerging adults. The work is a result of Nicholas's passion for emerging adults as well as his intellectual acumen to recognize the problem, develop a strategy and offer a plan of implementation to assist in alleviating the challenge that young adults face within the church community. The anticipated recommendations of implementation were reached due to the conclusions that were drawn in the research that was conducted. Therefore, the recommendations that are made to decrease retention and attraction of young adults was based on practical experiences and research conducted as opposed to solely relying on theoretical designs.

Refilling the Church's Fountain of Youth is a must read for any individual who has a need for grasping a further understanding of why the decline is occurring within churches amongst the young adult population. Therefore, pastors, church leaders and the emerging population are encouraged to add this work to their repertoire to further enhance their knowledge and wisdom of the challenges that exist within retention and attraction of young adults. Additionally, the work provides the example of a strong church community that understands the benefits of providing the young adults with support, love and the freedom to develop into disciples without fear of judgment or contradiction. Finally, the work is designed to provide assistance to any denomination or church that has recognized the decline of membership as it relates to emerging adults. It is indeed a necessary tool that can provide assistance and guidance for anyone working in the trenches of ministry.

Lori D. Spears, D.Min.
Associate Minister
Mount Ararat Baptist Church, Pittsburgh, PA

PREFACE

Refilling the Church's Fountain of Youth came into being as the result of my sojourn through my doctoral studies at United Theological Seminary in Dayton, Ohio as part of the Preaching and Leadership cohort. In the program, the school led doctoral students down a path of self-discovery that when examined in light of our ministry contexts at the time shed light on a problem for which we were uniquely suited to address. For me, this reflection and discovery shed light on the distinct challenge of the church to attract and retain emerging adults. I was uniquely positioned to take on this challenge after becoming serious in my Christian commitment, answering the call to preach, and ascending to leadership within my context (specifically leading youth and young adults) while being an emerging adult without a supportive ministry for these years.

This book adds my voice to the conversation of emerging adult attraction and retention. My voice is not only informed by my journey during emerging adulthood, but also by my experience as a youth and young adult ministry leader for more than ten years. These years of experience include innumerable conversations with emerging adults about what concerns them. However, research in several areas served to reinforce ideas implanted by personal experience. This book offers hope for churches with regard to their struggle to attract and retain young adults. I pray that the blueprint contained within these pages blesses congregations for years to come.

ACKNOWLEDGEMENTS

    I would like to utilize this space to thank my family and friends for their support and patience in this process. I am grateful to the Silas First Baptist Church and Pastor Jesse Young for their participation and the privilege of using this church the context for ministry model implementation. I am grateful to my contextual associates who helped me shape this model including Dominique Cross, Trevor Finney, Keonya Smith, and Chelsie Taliaferro. I am also appreciative to my former co-laborer in youth and young adult ministry in the person of Rev. Tracey Cherry who offered her support in my academic endeavors.

    I would also like to express gratitude to my mentors Terry Thomas, D.Min. and Reginald Dawkins, D.Min. for their guidance, support, encouragement, feedback, empowerment and instruction over the course of the Doctor of Ministry program that served as the primary source for this book. Along these same lines I thank my professional associates Faith Harris, D.Min., Harold Knight, D.Min., and Lester McCorn, D.Min. for their contributions. I also owe a debt of gratitude to my editor Lori D. Spears, D.Min. for her masterful editorial work in editing and in her eloquent presentation of the foreword for this book.

    Last but certainly not least, I want to acknowledge and thank my peers of the Preaching and Leadership group whose support, love, encouragement, and friendship have been invaluable to me. In particular, I want to single out my brothers and sister with whom I graduated including Drs. Scottie Aaron, Corey Brown, Angela Smith-Peeples, and Reginald Wells.

DEDICATION

This work is dedicated to my nuclear family and my family of origin. More specifically, I dedicate this to my wife Tanesha and our four children: Brenton, Brielle, Braeyen, and Brooklan. In addition, this work is dedicated to my parents James Meade, Sr. and Myra Meade along with my older brother James Meade, Jr. To both families, without your support I could not have made it and without you I would not be who I am. Thank you and I thank God for you.

For surely I know the plans I have for you, says the Lord, plans for your welfare and not for harm, to give you a future with hope.

– Jeremiah 29:11 NRSV

INTRODUCTION

One of the issues that have plagued the church for the past couple of decades is the issue of emerging adult attraction and retention. In other words, in my experience and as documented in other studies, it has been difficult for the church to draw and keep emerging adults or young adults between the ages of eighteen and thirty (hereafter emerging adult and young adult will be used interchangeably for referencing this specific group). The Model of Ministry therefore aimed at increasing the sense of relevance for the church with the hopes that this would present ingredients necessary for a ministry to attract and retain emerging adults. While many churches seem to focus their ministries and programs on the needs of children on one hand with those of middle-aged persons and senior citizens on the other, this Model of Ministry focused on defining what constitutes relevant ministry for emerging adults. While many uphold the children to be the future and those older than emerging adults the present and past, churches neglect to see that within emerging adulthood lie the more immediate successors of church ministry.

The pages that follow repeatedly use several words and phrases throughout. For the purpose of clarity, these terms should be defined clearly here. The term emerging adults for the purpose of this work includes young adults between the ages of eighteen and thirty. The model chose this descriptor to avoid the trap of focusing on a particular generation with the hope that this work and the principles it outlines can have an enduring impact upon churches and their efforts to minister to this critical demographic. Relevance in this context essentially means that something matters or bears importance most often to emerging adults. For example, relevant topics or issues for emerging adults refer to topics or issues that matter to young adults between the ages of eighteen and thirty. Also, the work references community frequently. Community for the purposes of the model of ministry is a spirit of synergy among a group of people who have some sense of relationship among them. In this case, a community of emerging adults involves a group of emerging adults working together in this group relationship. Openness, for the purposes of this work, means transparency and a willingness to be vulnerable enough to freely share honest opinions, beliefs, and feelings. As seen later, an example of this includes openness on the part of participants who honestly and freely share their stories with each other. Holistic refers to the nature of ministry that addresses persons' wellbeing in all areas of their lives such as physical, emotional, etc. and not simply spiritual.

In systematic fashion, this work lays critical foundations for this effort before discussing what happened, examining the results, and pondering a way forward for such ministry to emerging adults. The first chapter defines the ministry focus by expounding upon the problem that pervades many churches—the problem of emerging adult attraction and retention. This happens after the chapter discusses in detail my spiritual journey. Then this chapter leverages my experiences and discusses helpful perspectives on emerging adult ministry. Chapter One continues by examining issues that may often contribute to the at-large absence of young adults from many churches.

Chapter Two articulates a biblical foundation for this ministry using selected passages from both the Old Testament and New Testament. For each passage, the foundation discusses how the details in each passage support the design of the model of ministry. An examination of these texts yields a wealth of information as to the appropriate appearance of relevant ministry for emerging adults. This foundation begins with the Old Testament text by covering King Hezekiah's efforts to attract people to come to Jerusalem to celebrate the Passover in Second Chronicles the thirtieth chapter. After using the media of that era (letters) to communicate with the people, Hezekiah's message faces rejection from most but has success with others. Those who come do so in great numbers according to the writer and they have such a great time that they do not want the experience to end. Hezekiah's methods, process, and outcome provided inspiration and undergirding for the model of ministry. The New Testament foundation involves Acts 2:41-47 wherein engagement in holistic ministry kept new converts in Jerusalem, but also successfully attracted and added persons to the church. This foundation argues that relevant preaching or proclamation and relevant community bear the blame for the apostles' success. In both cases, the ministry that took place attracted and retained people of faith who were committed to God.

Chapter Three describes a historical foundation for the model of ministry by using the story of Perpetua, an emerging adult Carthaginian martyr, to support the use of holistic ministry within a supportive community to undergird emerging adult Christian faith. This chapter tells how she found support in her community and how this enabled and empowered her to hold on to her faith even under the threat of death. Her steady resolve provided inspiration as to how a supportive community that allows for ministry to the entire person could bring relevance to the Christian faith the members of the community profess. If these elements aided in her faith development and encouraged her as an emerging adult then, this chapter argues that these elements could accomplish the same in today's context.

The next chapter, four, discusses a theological foundation for the model of ministry and utilizes liberation theology for this purpose. This chapter uses the views of Gustavo Gutierrez and Leonard Boff to argue the necessity of the ethic of supportive community, especially found in ecclesial base communities, for relevant emerging adult ministry. Liberation theology, with its emphasis on theology in praxis and ministry to the entire person, suitably supports the model of ministry from a theological perspective as it holds that God is on the side of the oppressed and, therefore, God cares about a person's entire wellbeing. In addition, liberation theology at its core is an effort to make theology relevant to a particular community, which in this case is the community of the oppressed. The mobilizing effect that this theology had on Latin America therefore is helpful in finding theological underpinnings for the model of ministry.

After providing a theological foundation, this work then sets its aim on giving readers a theoretical foundation for the model of ministry in chapter five. This foundation utilizes sources outside of theology, including developmental psychology, in order to support both the need and practice for the model of ministry. The chapter also attempts to help the reader in understanding the special place in life that emerging adults occupy as well as the importance in reaching them at this critical juncture. This chapter cites and engages with many sources with regard to the place of faith in the lives of emerging adults as well as with regard to the problem of emerging adults leaving the church or abandoning faith and proposed solutions. This chapter also utilizes these sources to build support for the design of the model of ministry and for targeting an increased sense of relevance as a measurement.

After the previous four chapters present foundation for the model of ministry, chapter six discusses in detail the methodology behind the model design, describing the model of ministry and its results, as well as providing a final summary, reflection and conclusion. The first of these sections describes the type of study as being phenomenological utilizing source data triangulation with the help of observations, questionnaires, and interviews. In addition it provides the reader with all necessary background information for the study such as biases involved and the process for analysis. After this, the chapter presents the results and major findings discovered at the conclusion of the model of ministry. Immediately after this, the chapter reflects on the model of ministry while discussing potential changes for future implementations before summarizing the results or the nature of success and concluding. In the end this work examines a portable and repeatable model of ministry. While imagined and designed with emerging adults in mind, ministry leaders and pastors could easily apply the recipe this book provides to teaching ministries within the church. This valuable tool can be used by teachers in the church and classrooms and is not limited to any particular denomination or congregations comprised largely of any one ethnic group. This is the reason behind the book's title as it is a model for *the* church and provides a strategy for a refilling of *the* church's fountain of youth.

CHAPTER ONE
ARRIVING AT THIS FOCUS OF MINISTRY

My journey began at birth that came on October 19, 1980 at Johns Hopkins Hospital in Baltimore, Maryland. This arrival completed the nuclear family that began with married parents and an older brother. At the age of nine or ten our mother began bringing us to church on a consistent basis after her church's selection of a new pastor. Shortly after forcing us to attend church, our mother directed us to walk down the aisle and join the church in spite of the fact that we lacked understanding concerning the implications of this action. Shortly after, our mother enlisted us into various activities such as the youth choir, which at the time was the only activity for youth at the church other than Sunday school.

After some time passed the pastor of the church baptized my brother and me. Over the course of several years, the gospel became interesting, but being committed faithful to God and to the title of

Christian remained elusive with hypocrisy being preferred. Fear of our mother singularly fueled our participation in church activities. The salvation of my father only served to make the household stricter and increased our church workload to include ushering, singing and assisting in leading devotion. However, in spite of all of this activity, the feeling of a commitment to God only came after a personal moral failure during the junior year in high school, which was accompanied with intense and sincere godly sorrow. This godly sorrow did not linger nor translate into prolonged holy living.

While this change was temporary, in the spring of 1999 a more permanent commitment came during freshman year in college. After taking time for self-examination and self-reflection on the subject of character did unhappiness arise due to the evident character flaws. Furthermore, it was then that it became obvious that only God had the power to transform in order to produce God's intended design. These moments of reflection led to a full and complete commitment to God who was then given permission to initiate the transformation. God began making changes and my peers witnessed this transformation to the extent that they even noticed and commented on the newfound omission of profanity from everyday speech.

Like many others of prior generations, school led me away from my church. Upon returning to my home church, evidently only me and my best friend "Bobby" of our generation had been transformed and were committed to remaining a part of the church in our college years. We stayed primarily because of our individual commitments to God because at that time there were no programs or ministries geared toward meeting the needs of young adults from the age of eighteen to thirty. Being in community with another young adult, helped me in my pursuit of pleasing God. Soon after, "Bobby" would answer the call to preach—four years prior to my own call to do the same.

One of the greatest moments of my life was my call to the preaching ministry. My call first began to take shape in the form of the external call through a dream of one of my aunts. In the dream she saw me wearing a robe and initially interpreted the dream to mean that my career would include a judgeship before determining that the dream meant that my future included becoming a preacher. Resistance and denial was the initial response when the dream was shared outside of my friend's high school graduation. Despite my denial, others in my ministerial context made comments about my potential and repeatedly asked about my calling. One Sunday morning while leading worship, a conversation focusing on the goodness of God came out of my mouth, it was through multiple experiences such as this one that my call became solidified. Only later in life did God's will for my life become clear. Hearing a sermon compelling the people to seek God's will for their lives led to an earnest supplication for revelation concerning God's will for my life.

About two weeks later, "Bobby" invited me to attend his godfather's church, which facilitated my learning of a coming call to preach and teach. The development stage spanned over a four-year period. During the summers spent in Austin finding a suitable church seemed impossible which led to conducting services in the bedroom of my apartment. These services included playing gospel music before reading scripture and writing sermons even though a personal call to preach had not yet been answered. The early years of emerging adulthood served as the chronological setting for an entry into church leadership through the Youth and Young Adult Ministry. In May 2003, just prior to graduating from the University of Maryland at College Park, it became obvious that something was missing in spite of enjoying wonderful worship experiences. This led to the feeling of a great burden that prevented me from feeling completely fulfilled even in the midst of great worship. It occurred to me that was the call to the ministry so my pastor entertained questions concerning how the call to preach would feel.

After diligent prayer and reflection, it became clear that this void likely resulted from a lack of recognition of and not answering the call to preach. On a particular Sunday, which was either Mother's Day or the Sunday prior, it occurred to me that this emptiness or burden resulted from the call to preach. Opening my Bible followed a prayer asking God for confirmation. It was the fourteenth chapter of Joshua that ushered me into acceptance of my call. In this chapter Caleb praised God because he remembered the promise of the Promised Land and he acknowledged the fact that he made it to the Promised Land. Rereading this text became necessary due to a preliminary incorrect reading that believed that the text reported that Caleb was still waiting on the promise causing me to believe that this was not the call. The Spirit told me to read it again leading me to embracing the possibility of God's promise for me just like Caleb who arrived in the Promised Land.

The call was certain. Therefore, answering the call of God to preach the gospel took place through prayer. Prior to discussing this with anyone, my fasting endured three days in order to obtain reassurance concerning my call. After this, in a meeting my pastor received me well and expressed excitement when he became informed of my answering the call to preach. That night, following service, came the sharing of the news of the acceptance of the call to preach with my mother and father. While my father limited his response to a few words, he expressed that it was good news. My mother, however, expressed concern that this was the result of others who were pushing me to the call to ministry. She changed her tune following an assurance of an understanding of the gravity of this decision and that others would not be permitted to push me into the ministry. On July 6, 2003 came the initial sermon about two months after graduating with a bachelor of science degree, I solidified my place as a licensed associate minister. In addition, I cut my teeth as an assistant to the pastor, ministerial mentor, Sunday school teacher and a co-leader of the youth and young adult ministry. From humble beginnings up through the present various persons, relationships and pivotal moments helped position me to make a difference in the church all without the assistance of a supportive emerging adult ministry for those years of formation.

Barriers to Emerging Adult Ministry

If the church of model implementation is any indication, people thirty-five to sixty-five years of age make up the majority of church adult populations. By far the area of most concern due to its anemic population is the group aged between eighteen and thirty. When many depart the church in order to attend college or depart because their parents no longer force them to come, among other reasons, these young people often do not return or only return later in life. Perhaps becoming a leader in my early emerging adult years led me to be among the few within this age bracket who remain faithful and who have never departed.

Emerging adults face a number of barriers which may lead to their absence from many churches. These barriers include a conservative and literal approach to biblical studies where exegesis is ignored and context is taken for granted. In addition, like my own church, many other churches no longer serve the communities in which they sit. In these cases persons from the community leave to attend church and persons outside of the community commute into the community simply to go to church. When this is true, the church becomes separated from the community and perhaps no longer focused on the needs or ills of the community. Other emerging adults find no place for their creative expression in worship particularly in contexts where the liturgy is traditional, stale, and rejecting of more contemporary forms of worship. In addition, young adults are isolated from leadership positions. Add to this, the fact that as they become more educated these educated emerging adults must face the prospect of sitting under the leadership of uneducated or untrained pastors and leaders. In many cases, such leaders lack the tools to address in depth the theological questions and concerns of emerging adults.

At the same time, some churches have become proficient at using fear as an effective weapon for manipulating persons to get them to fall in line with certain lines of thinking. Doctrinally speaking, too often the church uses fear to motivate persons to live in fear of what God may do and withhold from persons because of their mistakes instead of believing that love is a greater motivator than fear. The church encourages congregants to strive to live like Jesus with the understanding that perfection is not attainable. However, it seems that many in the church hesitate to offer forgiveness to those who have fallen. Instead, many seem to prefer pointing and gossiping over restoring persons to proper fellowship and relationship with God.

There seems to be an emphasis within the church on identifying types of sin or stigmatizing particular sins. While fundamentally many churches promotes the idea that "sin is sin," or that all sin is equally condemned before God, based on my observation it seems that many repeatedly mention only certain sins. Those within the church have stigmatized these particular sins such as fornication, adultery, homosexuality and teenage or out-of-wedlock pregnancies. These sins have become scapegoats for the congregation who use them to steer conversations about sin away from the sins with which the majority struggles. Societal ills and evils, such as genocide and poverty, do not seem to get as much attention within congregations. Sadly, some churches persist in failing to address social issues outside pastoral commentary. When the pastor or visiting ministers broach such topics, members nod in assent and say amen in agreement, but it does not seem to necessarily translate into a zeal for social change. As a result, some who are now between the ages of eighteen and thirty who were raised in some churches still struggle with how to thrive in our society as evidenced by their dabbling in illegal activity and the inability to find careers.

Potential for Growth

Even for those persons, who like me, committed their lives to God during their young adult years there exists no ministry in place in many churches to specifically minister to those between the ages of eighteen to thirty. The church failed to establish a ministry for those persons before they transitioned from teenagers to young adults. It is possible, that similarly to me, the young people took an interest in the gospel, but only played the part of being a Christian that lured them away from the church. It is possible that the young adults became involved in church activities because they feared the persons who enlisted them in such activities. As a result, when these young adults became independent, they made the decisions to depart due to a lack of commitment to the church, the Christian faith or both. In addition, the absence of the young adults between the ages of eighteen to thirty also means that in the event that someone in this age bracket joined this church, they would not find a support community made up of their peers.

The assumption is that the young people of today are more accepting of people whose faith differs from their own and who live what some refer to as alternative lifestyles such as homosexuality. Traditional teaching also seems to have less of a hold on young people so that they are more open minded when it comes discussing their beliefs about God. As a result the young adults find themselves less comfortable in an atmosphere where older Christians have become consumed with a hamartiology that identifies and stigmatizes those things they believe to be sinful based on their narrow and literal interpretations of scripture. Furthermore, it is possible that young people, having been educated in areas such as science, no longer subscribe to traditional teachings after examining them vigorously. This generation seems to be more likely to believe the scientific theories that undergird the conservative interpretations of the Bible.

Furthermore, if people are going to feel sufficiently connected and committed to the church and their Christian faith, the theology set forth by the church to these persons cannot be as narrow as it has been presented in the past. In other words, it is believed that many people desire a holistic theology that paints God as caring about the needs of the whole person. The world in which these young people have been raised includes societal ills and evils such as world hunger, genocide, poverty and homelessness. A church that promotes a holistic theology, therefore, would address these issues thereby reflecting the image of God who cares about the needs of the whole person. This means that an evangelism that appeals to persons becoming complete in various areas would be more effective than one that simply focuses on salvation from the power and penalty of sin. Preaching and teaching specifically in the church should concern itself with persons' holistic liberation. God cares about the whole person and this conclusion came as the result of growth experienced in seminary.

My belief holds that emerging adults covet a support system from which they can benefit while at this context and a support system that also supports them from afar. In my opinion, these young people require a welcoming and nurturing context in which they can feel accepted and given the space to grow. In my mind, these young adults will benefit from a ministry that equips them to manage the struggles in life for college students. Additionally, having been the beneficiary of being surrounded with a community of faith, it would be beneficial for the ministry to assist in preparation for when entering the workforce. The community of faith was a place where persons never sought to influence my beliefs, but instead empowered him to discover "self" and provided a safe space for me to interrogate my beliefs. Seminary provided a context for the possibility of making life-long friends. This experience led to my development of other valuable relationships with people who could challenge and push me to higher heights in church-based ministry and the ministry of the academy. In this environment, embracing my identity and ability while growing became possible. Seminary helped me to understand that my greatest potential had not yet been reached. A similar environment should be of great benefit to persons within this demographic of eighteen to thirty year old adults.

The reason for my attachment to this concept, aside from those reasons previously provided, is that persons in this group find themselves at a critical juncture in their development not only as adults, but also as Christians. Having a supportive older brother and mentors in the faith, it is understandable how people in this age group could need unconditional support. For me, this also demonstrates the extent to which young adult Christians need the support of those willing to be their sisters and brothers keepers. Having only my best friend to share in the pursuit of holiness proved that committed persons in this age group desperately need to be surrounded with other godly individuals for moral support. This is in part because, persons who seek to live godly lives particularly at this stage of their lives often find themselves surrounded with peers who do not possess similar morals or who lack similar intentions. In other words, in order to lead these young adults toward holistic wellness, the targeted persons should feel as if they are a part of a family or community consisting of persons who aim only for their edification.

Moving those in the church in this direction requires leadership from a person who has benefited from such a nurturing environment. It also requires a leader who operates and is willing to continue operating in transparency or being honest about the leader's imperfections and shortcomings so that these young people have a leader with whom they can identify. In the same vein, leading this effort should only be assigned to one who has lived through these critical years and who has remained faithful to the ministry—a person whose personal faith in God still persists. This means that this leader should be familiar with what it takes to remain faithful and should be counted among them who have overcome the struggles of being a Christian in college. Furthermore, this leader should understand the difficulties of living a Christian life of integrity when living independently both in college and after entering the workforce. It is my belief that in order to meet this challenge, a leader must possess tools with regard to preaching, teaching and pastoral care. Such a leader should possess charisma and the ability to inspire these young people to be committed Christians who care about ministering to the whole person. Furthermore, this effort is only fit for a person who makes clear my unwavering commitment to these young people and to the faith.

The hope of the ministry as designed was to provide the best hope for attraction and retention of emerging adults by increasing their sense of relevance of the church. Reviving this demographic within this church would transform the context by injecting differing skillsets, new ideas and youthful energy into the ministry. The hope was that seeing a greater relevance for the church in the lives of young adults will lead to an increase in the number of young adults attracted to and retained by the church. According to my initial hypothesis, creating an inclusive community where preaching and teaching addresses the holistic concerns of young adults will lead to young adults to see greater relevance for the church in their lives. In regard to the church this work seeks to answer in the affirmative the question asked of the black church but better suited to the entire church and that is can the "church regain her relevancy among the young adults challenged and spiritually hungry generation?"[1] In the chapter that follows, this work presents a foundation for the approach to addressing this challenge through the lens of scripture.

NOTES

[1] Benjamin Stephens III and Ralph C. Watkins, foreword in *From Jay-Z to Jesus: Reaching and Teaching Young Adults in the Black Church* (Valley Forge, PA: Judson Press, 2009), vii.

CHAPTER TWO
BIBLICAL EXEMPLARS OF EFFECTIVE MINISTRY

Now that the book has provided background information concerning the problem that many churches face, it is only natural to look to the Bible in order to find stable footing for an approach to this problem's solution. The aim of this chapter is to examine ancient paradigms from scripture that move the church toward addressing a contemporary challenge of emerging adult attraction and retention—a demographic noticeably absent from churches at large. Both texts stress God's ethic in that God cares about the whole person and that members of the community should look out for the holistic wellbeing of others within their community. Many churches lack such a community for the targeted demographic, and focus only the spiritual while neglecting the need for relevant ministry that focuses on their holistic concerns or the concerns of the whole person.

Old Testament Foundation

The Old Testament scripture is Second Chronicles 30:1-13, 21-27 and it states,

> Hezekiah sent word to all Israel and Judah, and wrote letters also to Ephraim and Manasseh, that they should come to the house of the LORD at Jerusalem, to keep the Passover to the LORD the God of Israel. For the king and his officials and all the assembly in Jerusalem had taken counsel to keep the Passover in the second month (for they could not keep it at its proper time because the priests had not sanctified themselves in sufficient number, nor had the people assembled in Jerusalem). The plan seemed right to the king and all the assembly. So they decreed to make a proclamation throughout all Israel, from Beer-sheba to Dan, that the people should come and keep the Passover to the LORD the God of Israel, at Jerusalem; for they had not kept it in great numbers as prescribed. So couriers went throughout all Israel and Judah with letters from the king and his officials, as the king had commanded, saying, "O people of Israel, return to the LORD, the God of Abraham, Isaac, and Israel, so that he may turn again to the remnant of you who have escaped from the hand of the kings of Assyria. Do not be like your ancestors and your kindred, who were faithless to the LORD God of their ancestors, so that he made them a desolation, as you see. Do not now be stiff-necked as your ancestors were, but yield yourselves to the LORD and come to his sanctuary, which he has sanctified forever, and serve the LORD your God, so that his fierce anger may turn away from you. For as you return to the LORD, your kindred and your children will find compassion with their captors, and return to this land. For the LORD your God is gracious and merciful, and will not turn away his face from you, if you return to him." So the couriers went from city to city through the country of Ephraim and Manasseh, and as far as Zebulun; but they laughed them to scorn, and mocked them. Only a few from Asher, Manasseh, and Zebulun humbled themselves and came to Jerusalem. The hand of God was also on Judah to give them one heart to do what the king

and the officials commanded by the word of the LORD. Many people came together in Jerusalem to keep the festival of unleavened bread in the second month, a very large assembly. The people of Israel who were present at Jerusalem kept the festival of unleavened bread seven days with great gladness; and the Levites and the priests praised the LORD day by day, accompanied by loud instruments for the LORD. Hezekiah spoke encouragingly to all the Levites who showed good skill in the service of the LORD. So the people ate the food of the festival for seven days, sacrificing offerings of well-being and giving thanks to the LORD the God of their ancestors. Then the whole assembly agreed together to keep the festival for another seven days; so they kept it for another seven days with gladness. For King Hezekiah of Judah gave the assembly a thousand bulls and seven thousand sheep for offerings, and the officials gave the assembly a thousand bulls and ten thousand sheep. The priests sanctified themselves in great numbers. The whole assembly of Judah, the priests and the Levites, and the whole assembly that came out of Israel, and the resident aliens who came out of the land of Israel, and the resident aliens who lived in Judah, rejoiced. There was great joy in Jerusalem, for since the time of Solomon son of King David of Israel there had been nothing like this in Jerusalem. Then the priests and the Levites stood up and blessed the people, and their voice was heard; their prayer came to his holy dwelling in heaven.[1]

Introduction

In Second Chronicles 30:1-27, King Hezekiah leads the people in celebrating the Passover. Hezekiah reigned from circa 715-686 B.C.E. as king of Judah "during part of the time that Isaiah and Micah ministered as prophets in Judah."[2] The author of this book (hereafter referred to as the Chronicler) depicted "Hezekiah as the faithful successor of David who restored the religion of his nation after the lapse under Ahaz."[3] In other words, as soon as he ascended to the throne he was interested in getting the people back to being in faithful relationship with God. Hezekiah was a man of integrity who was only "twenty-five when he succeeded his father."[4] At the time of this religious renewal, Hezekiah according to today's standard was a young adult. He demonstrated that it was possible for a young adult to lead others. King Hezekiah was effective in leading others by extending a clarion call that attracted the people to come back to the city and into the sanctuary to celebrate the Passover. Hezekiah's actions and the results he received provided a suitable biblical foundation for the attraction and retention of young adults.

Contextual Analysis

In reference to the nomenclature of Chronicles, its title in Hebrew means "events of history" and its Greek title from the Septuagint means "things left over."[5] Its English name comes from the "Latin of Jerome" who entitled the volume "*Chronicon* of the Whole of Sacred History."[6] With regard to the identity of the Chronicler, there exists no consensus. Some scholars believe in the common authorship of Chronicles and Ezra-Nehemiah but one scholar wrote that she "came to the conclusion that Chronicles and Ezra-Nehemiah are two distinct works which were not, and could not have been, written by the same man."[7] Similarly to the issue of authorship, one finds no consensus among scholars who date the composition of this book anywhere from 529-200 B.C.E.[8] According to Rosenbaum's analysis, "the Chronicler's description of Hezekiah (2 [Chronicles] 29:1-32:33) was compiled soon after 520 B.C.E. In any case, Chronicles must be placed in the post-Exilic era when the luster of Josiah's temporary successes had faded."[9] However, "all recognize (the Chronicler's) debt to the writer of Joshua through Kings, though they admit that the Deuteronomistic work as we have it was by no means his only source."[10]

The book of Chronicles is a narrative but its genre is historical.[11] More specifically, Japhet wrote that "(Chronicles) is a work of historiography, an account of Israel's history from its beginning until the destruction of the First Temple."[12] Therefore, it is fitting that it completes the section of the Old Testament referred to as history along with the book of Esther.[13] However, in the Hebrew Bible, Chronicles follows Ezra and Nehemiah and is in the "canonical division called Writings."[14] In the English Bible before this book lies the first volume of Chronicles followed by Ezra. The selected passage falls within the second volume of Chronicles and is sandwiched between chapters that deal with religious reforms. One scholar appropriately labeled this passage "Hezekiah's Passover."[15] The text itself may be divided into two parts: "preparation for the Passover (vv. 1-12) and then its celebration (vv. 13-27)."[16] For the purposes of this foundation, the text will be divided into six parts: the plan for the Passover (verses 1-5), the decree and the invitation to the remnant (verses 6-9), the response to the invitation (verses 10-13), a desire to continue the festivities (verses 21-23), and the worshipping community (verses 24-27).

Detailed Analysis

Clearly, "The Chronicler attaches great significance to the Passover."[17] With regard to the "spiritual temperature" of Hezekiah's generation, the "flames of enthusiasm for God had nearly disappeared among the people of God."[18] Verses one through five discuss the people's plan for celebrating the Passover. Beginning with verse one, it becomes clear to Hahn that "Hezekiah is deeply convinced that God's people must 'keep the Passover to the LORD the God of Israel,' and he believes it to be his solemn duty as king to ensure a faithful observance by all Israel (30:1)."[19] This sense of duty followed by sincere action demonstrated Hezekiah's leadership—he was not simply a leader through title, but a leader through action. With regard to Hezekiah's motives for calling for the Passover to be celebrated, Feldman writes that "Josephus explains that Hezekiah's motive was not the political aggrandizement that one might have suspected—namely, that he was seeking that they might become subject to him against their will—but rather true piety, in that he was striving for their own good and happiness."[20] Leadership is not about leveraging other people to promote one's own glory, but instead through Hezekiah's example one is able to see that leadership is working for the good of the individuals that they lead.

Furthermore, Hahn writes that, "to these northern tribes the Chronicler issues a heartfelt call to homecoming. Their true home, he wants them to know, is Jerusalem."[21] One could also argue that Hezekiah used a different method for reaching the tribes of Ephraim and Manasseh than he did for the elder tribes. In other words, his methodology differed with regard to reaching the new generation as Ephraim and Manasseh were the sons of Joseph, one of Jacob's original twelve sons. At the same time, "Hezekiah's Passover is commonly regarded as an anachronism,"[22] but according to another scholar time the "observance's lack of orthodoxy" detailed in verses two through four of this chapter give credence to the idea that this account is authentic.[23] Hezekiah and the people decided to hold the Passover feast in the second month rather than the first according to verse two. According to Simeon Chavel, the circumstances surrounding its delay reflected at least in part the "lethargy of the priests and the apathy of the people."[24] In other words deficiencies with the leaders and the people they led prompted Hezekiah's delay. To Humphrey this demonstrated that "Hezekiah knew that God cares more about grace than rules, more about people than policies."[25] Put another way, "for Hezekiah, the people and their relationship to God was more important than the rules."[26] In verse five, the Chronicler in effect reported that the appeal went throughout the "traditional boundaries of Israel."[27] "The use of 'Beersheba to Dan' should be viewed as a useful hendiadys for the full extent of the kingdoms."[28]

In verses six through nine, messengers spread Hezekiah's decree and invite the remnant to return to Jerusalem to celebrate the Passover through the use of letters or the media of the day. According to verse six, the "couriers travel the length of the country…trying to persuade people to make the pilgrimage."[29] In addition, the "letter that Hezekiah publishes throughout the land is filled with inner-biblical quotations and echoes. His immediate sources are the promises made by God and Solomon during the dedication of the temple."[30] Hahn further adds, "Hezekiah's form of address, 'O sons of Israel,' is used several times in the writings of the prophets to summon the exiled population to repentance and conversion."[31] Hezekiah's choice of words also deserves attention due to the fact that "in 722 or 721 the already much reduced northern kingdom of Israel was finally overrun by the Assyrians," and the occurrences accounted for in this pericope "clearly assume that the northern kingdom had already lost its independent existence."[32] Put another way the "Chronicler has already shown his awareness that even in the apostate northern kingdom might be found some loyal servants of God, and so here Hezekiah is pictured as appealing to any such, that they would return to true worship in Jerusalem."[33]

In verses seven and eight, "Hezekiah picks up this language in his letter, seemingly to describe the experience of the people of the north. Their ancestors and relatives, he says, were 'stiff-necked' and 'faithless…to the LORD God of their fathers' (2 Chr. 30:7-8). The expression 'the LORD God of their fathers' is not used often outside of Chronicles."[34] However, Hezekiah's word choice pointed to a holistic view of the kingdom. This is in part because the "great sin shared by both Israel and Judah (under Ahaz) is the abandonment of

Yahweh's sanctuary in Jerusalem (v. 8)."[35] By inviting both the North and the South, "in this moment the breach between north and south has been bridged. The sons of Israel are once more united in 'service'…to the Lord their God (30:8)."[36] According to Hezekiah "their true vocation is to worship the Lord in his temple."[37] The message stressed also the benefits of returning in verse nine to include compassion and the privilege of returning to their land. The message lastly stressed the grace and mercy of God who will not abandon them if they turn to God.

Verses ten through thirteen provide details concerning the various responses to the invitations. Verse ten notes that "Hezekiah's message is not generally well received among the remnant of Israel" and "his couriers are laughed to scorn and mocked (v. 10)."[38] But on a more positive note, the "candid description of Hezekiah's relatively unsuccessful appeal to the North support its authenticity."[39] Feldman offers that "Hezekiah's sincere piety is all the greater because the opposition that his envoys encountered was even more vicious than that described in the Bible (2 [Chronicles] 30:10), reaching the point where the Israelites actually killed their prophets."[40] To this McKenzie adds that the "response of the northerners (vv. 10-11) confirms the chronicler's view of them as apostate."[41] In contradistinction to the failure to reach those in verse ten, verse eleven suggests that others responded positively to the invitation and connects their positive response with the virtue of humility. This verse notes that humility was involved in these persons turning to God and responding positively to the invitation.

With regard to Hezekiah's success with some of the remnant, Feldman writes that "Josephus also exaggerates Hezekiah's success in convincing members of the tribes of Israel to come to Jerusalem. Thus, whereas the biblical text (2 [Chronicles] 30:11) states that only a few men of the tribes of Asher, Manasseh, and Zebulun came to Jerusalem as a result of Hezekiah's invitation and of his prophets' exhortations,

Josephus says both that many came and that they flocked...to Jerusalem to worship God."[42] While Hezekiah's success with the northern kingdom was limited, the text reports that the hand of God was upon Judah. In fact, "Judah, however, is united in enthusiastic response (v. 12)," and notes Hezekiah's effectiveness in getting his subjects to follow him.[43] These verses suggest that any invitation to religious exercise and commitment will receive a mix of rejection and acceptance but that a failure of many to accept the invitation does not doom the ministry nor diminish the joy experienced by those who participate. Verse thirteen and the verses that follow reveal a working partnership and collaboration between leadership and the worshipping community.

The final seven verses of this chapter, twenty-one through twenty-seven, reveal that the worshipping community desired more festivities. Verse twenty-one and twenty-two provides detail regarding the worshipful spirit of the community who kept the festival with joy. Verse twenty-two also discusses how Hezekiah, as an effective leader should, encouraged the Levites. Verse twenty-three informs its readers that the "Passover became such an exciting event that the people asked that it continue for a second week."[44] McKenzie rightly notes that the "prolonging of the celebration for a second week illustrates the people's exuberance and is reminiscent of the second week of celebration at the dedication of Solomon's temple" as well as "Hezekiah's provision of the offerings and the assembly of all Israel for the occasion."[45] Jarick adds that "this revivification of the temple services us such a success that, after the prescribed week of festivities has been completed, no one is willing to bring the experience to the end."[46] Hezekiah led the people by example in worship as noted in verse twenty-four where he gave a great number of animals to be sacrificed for offerings. As a leader, he possessed and presented what the people needed to participate and find relevance in worship.

Verse twenty-five describes the "true community" where "there is no spirit of exclusivism."[47] The ministry should seek to be inclusive in order to maximize the sense of community. In the next verse, the Chronicler expressed "the idea of an observance outdoing all that had previously taken place."[48] With regard verse twenty-six, "[Josephus] also increases even further the splendor…and magnificence…with which the Passover, under the inspired leadership of Hezekiah, was celebrated."[49] Verse twenty-seven communicates the splendor and greatness of the festival. In reference to this verse Hahn writes that the "Passover is vital to Israel's national identity and corporate memory; there is no question that for the Chronicler the Passover is the feast of the kingdom par excellence, the feast in which the people experience intimate communion with God, who blesses them through his priest and accepts their prayers in his holy habitation (30:27)."[50] In verse twenty-seven, it is clear that the people were "blessed by their religious leaders" who showed them to way to right relationship with God.[51]

Synthesis

This text communicates the ethic of godly leadership leading a community into religious renewal. This passage promotes the value of the worshipping community as well as the necessity for effective leadership in building and sustaining a community of faith. Hezekiah's techniques and strategies help the church today to understand what may be effective in creating such an environment to which participants do not want to say goodbye. In short, Hezekiah attracted and retained persons to the worshipping community at Jerusalem thereby providing an effective foundation for emerging adult attraction and retention.

Reflection

With regard to the "spiritual temperature" of Hezekiah's generation, the "flames of enthusiasm for God had nearly disappeared among the people of God."[52] As mentioned previously, just as the people's enthusiasm waned during Hezekiah's generation, this could also be said of the young adults in many churches where some enthusiasm remains, but not nearly as much as should be present. Just as Hezekiah showed leadership through moving as a result of his sense of duty, the context in question requires such leadership to be a catalyst for attracting and retaining emerging adults. Leaders also need to be flexible and Hezekiah showed such flexibility when he agreed to hold the Passover in the second month instead of the first. The timing of the request occurred because the normal schedule would not permit. It symbolizes the need to communicate to the people their intent to do something out of the ordinary. Humphrey writes "sometimes we need to make exceptions to the rules to minister more effectively to people as well as to generate momentum."[53] They did not want to wait an additional year almost; instead they decided to seize the day so as not to put off this religious reformation. As time goes on the church loses more young adults to other churches and to apostasy. Hezekiah's approach demonstrates the need for the model of ministry to seize the day in order to prevent more loss and increase the esteem of the young adults.

Hezekiah sent out widespread invitations and the pattern of casting a large net helps shape the model of ministry. Just as it was in the case of Hezekiah, a wide appeal is necessary in order to get young adults to return or come for the first time to the ministry. The lack of great numbers means that they had fallen away from keeping the Passover similarly to the way that young adults fall away from the church today. Just as Hezekiah acted so must leadership act to take the necessary steps to attract and retain emerging adults some of whom may include those who formerly belonged to churches before falling away.

Hezekiah used the media of the day to communicate with the various tribes to invite them to come to the house of the Lord at Jerusalem in order to keep the Passover. Hearkening back to the detailed analysis, it could be argued that Hezekiah used appropriate or relevant means to reach each demographic in order to get his message disseminated to all. Similarly to the function of the couriers in Hezekiah's day, emerging adults in churches and social media should be used to carry the invitation to emerging adults to come to churches for the purpose of participating in the model of ministry. One of the potential areas of growth in the many churches is the lack of communication that suits this new digital age. The church has some minimal social media exposure and a channel on YouTube, but the church has not updated its website in years. The model ministry should follow the pattern of Hezekiah in using the media today to communicate with young adults to include social media and blogs.

Hezekiah's model also is relevant in that this ministry should reach out to those members who formerly belonged to the church of model implementation prior to their falling away. As it was with Hezekiah's appeal to the northern kingdom, the model of ministry should be a ministry that seeks to persuade young adults to come to church and for some of them to return to the church. The emphasis in the appeal of the model ministry should then be what draws young adults together rather that which distinguishes them from others. The more of what they have in common is stressed the more successful the appeal would be and the stronger the sense of community. The model of ministry's invitations would not only appeal to emerging adults to come and to return, but like Hezekiah's these invitations would provide them with a rationale for why emerging adults should come to this church. Hezekiah invited them to come keep the Passover, thereby, sharing part of their national heritage with each other.

The model ministry, taking its cues from Hezekiah, would emphasize what young adults have in common as a means for attracting and retaining young adults. The lack of specific ministry for young adults and the potential for this ministry meeting that need would attract young adults to the church, but this news would have to be disseminated effectively. In the same way that Hezekiah invited the Samaritans to return to the fold, leadership is necessary specifically to invite persons who have no dealings with Christians or the church, or the unchurched, to come to church especially young adults. Hezekiah utilized language familiar with his audience to communicate the need for them to return. This model of ministry building on Hezekiah's foundation would also use language common with emerging adults in order to reach them.

The remnant of the northerners is symbolic of the remnant of emerging adults present in churches who remain in spite of the mass exodus or exile of others in this demographic. The remnant are those who symbolize the young adults in particular that have survived the dangers prevalent during emerging adult years to include prison, drugs, alcohol and other self-destructive habits. Hezekiah's message stressed returning to God so as to incur divine favor and stressed the faithlessness of many in their ancestry. In a similar way, the model of ministry's message would need to connect and communicate that the emerging adults in churches and beyond should not be like previous generations who abandoned the church during their emerging adult years. The model of ministry should reflect Hezekiah's model by also clearly communicating the holistic benefits of the ministry to emerging adults.

As the hand of God was upon Judah, so the hand of God must be involved in any ministry seeking to effectively attract and retain emerging adults. The mixed response that Hezekiah's invitations received likely predicts the success of the model of ministry with regard to attracting and retaining emerging adults along with the outcome that any rejection will not noticeably negatively affect the experience of those who attend. The young adults who reject the invitation to come or to stay may do so for the same reason that some of the northerners rejected Hezekiah's appeal—apostasy. As mentioned above, lethargic priests ended up leading apathetic people, and similarly leaders today must share part of the blame for the falling away of emerging adults by failing to make ministry relevant for them while at the same time possessing integrity.[54] While some have simply walked away from the church to attend churches more able to meet their holistic needs, others have walked away from the church completely. This model needs to have a realistic, but not pessimistic, expectation of the potential success of this model of ministry. Like Hezekiah, this model must also promote the virtue of humility in order to get emerging adults to submit to God and become faithful participants in the church of interest. Humility is especially necessary in order to get persons to return to this context after departing years ago. In summary, the couriers went out and shared the message, but were rejected and mocked. Some humbled themselves and came—symbolizing not everyone will be receptive to the message, but those that do have humbled themselves and returned home or to the church. Judah's positive response recorded in verse twelve showed that upon issuing an appeal effective leaders may succeed in getting positive responses from those that this model seeks to attract. As it was with Hezekiah, emerging adults need to partner with leadership in creating an environment such that emerging adults find relevance.

In the end, Hezekiah and his team succeeded so much so that the worshipping community did not want the festivities to end. Following his example makes possible the lofty goal of providing the necessary motivations and assurances to get emerging adults to come and to stay involved in a context of ministry implementation. One of the goals of the brief implementation of the model ministry is that persons will not want such a ministry to end, but will want it to continue after bringing such ministry back to life in the context of concern. They not only came, but they lingered not wanting the good times to end thereby symbolizing that attracting young adults and showing them such a fulfilling time in a spirit of community can make it so that they do not want to be without the experience. As it was with Hezekiah, this is possible in the midst of authentic community or an environment free from exclusivism as described in verse twenty-five.[55] Just as the religious leaders blessed the people in verse twenty-seven, similarly it would take strong leadership in order to effectively appeal to and minister to young adults already in churches and to those attracted to the context by a broad appeal.

By offering relevant ministry and maintaining corporate and individual integrity, churches and leaders of this ministry should be walking in Hezekiah's footsteps where he did not condemn the people, but provided thousands of animals on behalf of those who returned for the Passover as recorded in verse twenty-four. Hezekiah provided materials to ensure the participation of those who returned and the church must do the same by providing ministry and community that welcomes emerging adult participation. His example shows that ministry to emerging adults must offer relevant ministry led by a person of integrity in a context of integrity while offering relevant content and a non-judgmental community in which they can wrestle with their beliefs. Emerging adults, when using this passage as a biblical foundation, should be invited to participate in religious activities that get them to remember what God has already done. Hezekiah's methods while ancient have contemporary application for a context that requires religious renewal for the emerging adult portion of its congregation. Only by sending a clarion call, as it was in the case of Hezekiah will the church attract apostate and unchurched young adults alike. By commemorating God's previous activity, as this text shows, makes it possible to stir up the faith of the remnant of emerging adults who remain.

New Testament Foundation

However, no biblical foundation would be complete without also utilizing a text from the New Testament; a text that lifts up similar ideals with similar results. The New Testament text is Acts 2:42-47 and it states,

> They devoted themselves to the apostles' teaching and fellowship, to the breaking of bread and the prayers. Awe came upon everyone, because many wonders and signs were being done by the apostles. All who believed were together and had all things in common; they would sell their possessions and goods and distribute the proceeds to all, as any had need. Day by day, as they spent much time together in the temple, they broke bread at home and ate their food with glad and generous hearts, praising God and having the goodwill of all the people. And day by day the Lord added to their number those who were being saved (Acts 2:42-47).

Introduction

This particular passage of scripture chronicles the primitive years of the movement of the followers of Christ following his ascension. For "at Pentecost the people of God were re-created in community, and the church was born."[56] It paints the portrait of an ideal Christian community in which each member receives what he or she needs. This text therefore is a model of the ideal behavior of the community within today's churches. The model set forth in these verses promote the idea that Christians should not simply be self-absorbed, but instead be concerned with the holistic wellbeing of all those with whom they share the bond of faith in Jesus Christ. As one particular scholar put it, "these verses contain a highly idealized picture of the life of the early

Christian community and are as such one of the examples from late antiquity of idealizing descriptions of religious brotherhoods like the Essenes, Therapeutae, Brahmans, Gymnosophists, Egyptian priests, Pythagorean communities, etc."[57] In the Twentieth Century, "For Gentile Christians...Acts 2 is a profound reminder of the Jewish origins of the faith and of their dependence upon the faithful in Israel who have served as a light to the nations" according to Tiede.[58] The context for the model of ministry lacks the sense of togetherness described in these verses especially among persons aged eighteen to thirty.

Contextual Analysis

According to tradition Luke, who was likely a Gentile Christian, wrote this book along with the gospel of Luke.[59] Other sources suggest that while his name may be unknown, the author may be characterized as "an educated and well-traveled Greek" who may have been a Jewish proselyte before he became a Christian missionary.[60] For the sake of clarity, the remainder of this work will use Luke in place of the author. Reta Finger wrote, "the book of Acts is the second volume in Luke's two-volume work on the story of Jesus and the story of the church."[61] According to the early part of the gospel of Luke, the author dedicated the text to Theophilus and conveyed that the author wrote to illuminate Theophilus concerning the things of which Theophilus received prior instruction (Luke 1:3-4). The writer also addressed Theophilus in the book of Acts and it is logical that the author had the same purpose in mind (Acts 1:1). According to one source the purpose may be six-fold on the basis of the "distinctive theological emphases in Acts" including "irenic, polemical, apologetic, evangelistic, pastoral, and theological."[62]

Scholars continue to debate the question of the date and place of the origin of Acts. The book itself contains no clear indications of either the dating or geographical genesis of this book.[63] In fact, "the opinion among scholars about the date when Acts was written varies greatly, ranging all the way from as early as A.D. 57/59 to A.D. 150."[64] Possibly, the author wrote this book somewhere in the vicinity of 85 C.E. to 95 C.E. after writing Luke's gospel.[65] With regard to the place of composition, "Antioch of Syria and Rome are the most common suggestions for the provenance of Acts. Nevertheless, perhaps Luke intended his works for an audience without boundaries, as it was, in fact, widely distributed and appreciated from the beginning."[66]

In those times, "the only social security people had in that world was the extended family" where individuals were part of a "tight-knit clan" of economic equilibrium where persons would practice what is called "generalized reciprocity" except in the case of individual rejection by society.[67] This explains why circumstances forced persons who abandoned everything in their pursuit of following Jesus to organize their own "kin-group."[68] In other words, "the sort of thing Luke talks about in Acts 2 and 4 makes perfect sense if you understand how ancient Mediterranean community life is structured."[69] The members of the target demographic in the church of model implementation largely isolate themselves from one another thereby preventing this sort of synergy and mutual benefit of relationship. In fact, the independence rather than interdependence of these persons on each other could cause some to draw the conclusion that they do not believe that they need each other as was the case with the persons in this text.

In reference to source material, in both the cases of the gospel and the book of Acts, "Luke has edited his sources to show how the story of Jesus is paralleled in the story of the church, and vice versa."[70] In addition, according to the expertise of a particular scholar "source theories have been of four types: (1) the search for written sources, mainly in chapters. 1–15; (2) the specific question of whether an Aramaic original stands behind chapters. 1–15; (3) theories connected with the "we" narrative of chapters. 16–28; and (4) the possibility that Luke used primarily oral sources and isolated bits of local tradition."[71] Regardless of its sources, Acts is the fifth book of the New Testament and lies sandwiched between the four gospels and Pauline epistles. Within the book of Acts, one source places the passage of emphasis within a section entitled "The early Jewish church in Jerusalem (1:6-5:42)" and "the character and vigor of early Christian Judaism (1:9-5:42)."[72] Yet another source places this pericope within the section entitled "The Spirit Empowers the Church for Witness (1:1–2:47)" and entitles this passage "The Common Life of the Community (2:42–47)."[73]

Concerning the form of the book of Acts, one scholar sees it as a theological work like the gospels "whose message is contained in a setting of events and discourses."[74] Another notes that "Acts is usually assigned to the genre of "general history" and compared to other works in the Greco-Roman world that recorded the origins and progress of particular ethnic or national groups."[75] One expert says that the genre of this book is consistent with the gospel of Luke that is "alluded to in the preface to Acts (1:1-2)" in that it is the second volume of a historical narrative.[76] Based on observation, emerging adults within the church seem oblivious to the ethics, which undergirded the establishment of the church as recorded in texts like these.

One can also view the book of Acts as the first major summary according to one source where summaries filled the gaps between the author's "freestanding episodes."[77] Summaries within this book also "follow the tradition of providing an eclectic résumé of a specific community."[78] For the purposes of this chapter, the text will be divided into three parts: the church engaging in holistic ministry which benefits the church (verses 42-43), the church practicing an ethic of community and peer support (verses 44-47a), and the church grows after the creation of such a community (verse 47b).

Detailed Analysis

Luke's portrayal as being unwavering in the principal norms of church life "begins the pattern of idealization that marks all the summaries."[79] In other words this summary details the ideal pattern of behavior for the church. In this text they did not feel divided about doing what was best for the individual and what was best for the community because the two were in sync. Put another way, there existed a synergy in those days between doing what was in the individual's best interest and doing what was in the best interest of the Christian community. It makes sense then that monastic writings, including some by Augustine, "cite the Acts summaries in Chapters 2 and 4 as their basis for sharing the common life."[80] Beginning with verses forty-two and forty-three the church begins to engage in holistic ministry practices, such as signs and wonders in addition to teaching, fellowship, breaking of bread, and praying, that internally benefits the community. Sadly, the context on which the model focuses lacks many activities or practices which contribute toward meeting the overall goal of ministering to the needs of the whole person. This selection of text "allows us to identify four characteristics of these small groups: (1) community, (2) Bible study, (3) worship and prayer, and (4) outreach."[81]

Verse forty-two records that "they devoted themselves to the apostles' teaching and fellowship, to the breaking of bread and the prayers." The "they" in Acts 2:42 refers to the believers who responded in faith to Peter's first speech recorded earlier in this chapter after being "cut to the heart" by his words in the first part of this book. These were the first converts or the first disciples of the disciples. This is a template for a ministry that benefits disciples especially those new to the faith as it includes instruction, fellowship, eating together and praying. These activities had the purpose of strengthening the community and benefit each participant holistically. Only those persons who were already part of this community participated in the activities described in verse forty-two. Setran and Kiesling wrote, "these key components of early church life—teaching, fellowship, worship, and outreach—constitute a kind of 'curriculum' for the body, a holistic picture of the communal life of faith in the local congregation."[82] One of the issues for the context to address is that there exists no formal ministry to address the holistic needs of persons already committed to the faith. This is the case in spite of the fact that the activities described in the text became a quasi-support structure for these new converts. In contradistinction to the context in question, these persons observed the value and relevance of the message they received. One could think of this teaching of the apostles as "designate this teaching as theological reflection in dialogue aimed at deliberative and lived-out application."[83]

These activities included fellowship which in the Greek is a term called "*koinonia*." This term "connotes the bond of responsibility for one another enjoined on believers by their assent to the gospel."[84] As mentioned previously, it seems that the Christian members in the midst of emerging adulthood in churches do not feel this sense of responsibility to each other. However, the Christians described in the text also took part in the breaking of bread which can be considered the technical terminology for the Eucharist in Acts but "originally the ritual opening of a festive Jewish meal."[85] Communion provided a centering moment for this community because it reinforced the "reason for and the nature of its life together."[86] These were communal activities designed to be a blessing to the entire person. Here the new disciples expressed commitment to not only things which benefited them spiritually such as the apostles' teaching and prayer, but also to things which affected the body and the mind namely the breaking of bread and fellowship respectively. The disciples participated in these last two items as a community thereby communicating an inherent benefit to its communal existence. This body benefited from such a cooperative environment by having persons with whom they could express themselves in the faith. This ensured that no one particular member of the group felt isolated in his or her commitment to following the apostolic doctrine. In order for a particular group of believers to grow together and be effective this group must participate in these four activities. This explains the lack of growth within the targeted age group, as there exists no age-specific instruction, consistent fellowship, communal meals or formal prayer ministry such as intercessory prayer partners.

In the text, the apostles then perform signs and wonders as recorded in verse forty-three causing everyone to stand in awe or reverential fear. These signs and wonders served as a "consolidation of the credentials of the eschatological in which his witnesses collaborate with the risen Lord."[87] The signs and wonders take place because the apostles must provide evidence that this to which persons have committed themselves is real. The behavior of the apostles reinforced the beliefs and the commitment of the new converts to this movement. Churches should therefore continue in this apostolic tradition by supporting the faith of young adults instead of undermining their faith with disputes and debates over the church's teaching especially on controversial subjects such as alcohol consumption and sex. This ethic oftentimes seems absent from churches where older members do not necessary reinforce the faith of young adults as did the leadership of the converts described in the text.

In verse forty-four, it is apparent that the "parable of the Great Dinner in Luke 14, to which the most marginalized people were invited, was being fulfilled, along with Deuteronomy 15:4, which promised that in the New Age "there will be no one in need among you."[88] For Luke, "the promise of Deuteronomy is being fulfilled in the early church."[89] This verse speaks to the unity among the people who were so bonded in *koinonia* that they withheld nothing of need from their sisters and brothers in the community. Given the context of this book this is not surprising for "the idea of collective property (εἶχον ἅπαντα κοινά) has a long history in ancient Greek and Latin literature."[90] Van der Horst states, Acts 2:44 should be seen in this light "although it can not be denied that besides this Hellenistic motif also" the concept that Deuteronomy 15:4 "has been fulfilled in the early Christian community plays a role here."[91]

The foundation of their unity was their common belief in the same gospel. This supports the idea that faith in Christ is sufficient to cause persons to be committed to a community with persons who share this faith. This community possessed a sense of togetherness where it seemed to minimize differences and embrace commonalities. In verse forty-five, the writer reports that those in the community sold items and distributed the proceeds to meet everyone's need. The author thereby places emphasis on the selflessness of the members of the community who did what was necessary in order to assist their sisters and brothers in their deficiency. This symbolizes an emptying of persons and giving of themselves to the cause of others. This spirit of selflessness seems altogether absent from many young adults, including those in the church I used to test my model, in this age that do not seem inclined to do anything for the benefit of others from which actions they also benefit. One could argue that this lack of selflessness on the part of emerging adults finds its genesis in the observed selfishness of older adults who for the most part refuse to serve and in their behavior model a selfishness that limits the feeling of community in churches.

In verse forty-six, the text reports that this body of believers shared an ethic of community by how they related to each other. Toward the end of the passage, Luke reported that this community spent time together, but this means more than simply occupying the same space at the same time. In the Greek, the word for together literally means "with one mind."[92] On another note, "in Acts 2:46 we see that the Jerusalem church was divided into two mutually supportive meetings—a large-group meeting that expressed the Christians' corporate unity (meeting together in the temple courts) and more intimate small-group meetings (Breaking of bread in homes)."[93] Once again those within the community broke bread together or shared in meals from house to house. When combined with the previous point it is evident that this community practiced holistic ministry within. As a result, the pericope notes that those in the community had glad or generous hearts. In other words, this relationship among those within the community became a source of joy. The beginning of verse forty-seven also notes that they praised God suggesting that they thanked God for the lives that they enjoyed, and they fell in favor with those outside of the community as well. The young adults within churches would benefit greatly from a similarly supportive environment.

The end of verse forty-seven informs its readers of the fact that the community progressively grew numerically as more persons were saved or received the gospel message. Not only did these new believers join the church at large, but this specific community also admitted these new sisters and brothers of the faith. The text does not describe a hard link between the salvation of these new additions and this community, but it is possible that the behavior of this community did nothing to discourage salvation on the basis of undesirable characteristics or behaviors. It is possible that the behavior of this community played a role in encouraging persons to receive the gospel.

Perhaps some received salvation with the knowledge that one of the incentives was that this excellent community of believers who share similar experiences and issues was there waiting on them and willing to embrace them. These possibilities provide hope for addressing the shortcomings among the emerging adults within the church. The community described in this text provided a support system for these new Christian disciples and as a result served as one of, if not the first of, support ministries within the church body to act for the edification of individual believers.

Synthesis

The passage of Acts 2:42-47 provides an idealized description of the inner workings of the community consisting of Christian believers who act in each other's best interest. This text shows, theoretically, that it is possible for the church to establish communal structures that strictly exist for the purpose of edifying its Christian membership. While it may be true that the "danger in the Lukan summary is that we might be tempted to disparage the church today and to lift up the primitive church itself as the church's model for all time," the intent is to simply to utilize the principles found in this idealization of the Christian community.[94] The community is responsible for providing the elements, which will edify the membership to include teaching, fellowship and peer support. One result of the Christian believer having such a resource is the hardening of one's faith and the strengthening of one's commitment. This is possible when the community becomes a blessing to its members by ensuring that the body supplies the holistic needs of each person in the faith community. Community and the holistic ministry that it provides, according to this text, may serve as a precursor for the growth of said community.

Reflection

In a way this text serves as a type for ministries within the church who specifically minister to those who have already received, in faith, the gospel message. It typifies the sort of behavior, togetherness and support necessary for the church to continue to positively affect the persons within the church. The actions taken by leadership of this community should be such that they compel those being led to be in awe of God. This passage undergirds the notion that these persons eighteen to thirty will not become more committed without anointed and sent leadership. The model ministry is necessary because like those in verse forty-two of this passage, persons within the church need to have something in place which provides these elements—a ministry to which they feel compelled to devote themselves. The aim is to stimulate similar individual commitment through the establishment of such a ministry.

The model for this project depends on this particular passage because it shows what sound teaching when combined with community and holistic benefits motivates and galvanizes persons within the group participating in these activities. Similarly to the community portrayed in this text, teaching is critical in this model as a means to attract and nurture the targeted group.[95] As it was with communion, this ministry should serve as a centering place for the community. Community and holistic ministry include not only fellowshipping, praising God, and addressing spiritual needs, but also addressing physical needs and psychological needs for companionship and *koinonia*. This body shared the same space and time both inside and outside of the church. This sense of community is necessary to offset the predisposition in this society toward individualism for as Finger notes, "only in affluent Western cultures have we promoted individualism to such a degree that we can scarcely imagine such a communal lifestyle and worldview."[96]

This recipe produced the goodwill of all people and growth within both the church and the community. Knowing that a community of Christians aged eighteen to thirty provides an incentive for lost persons within this demographic to embrace the faith because they know they are not alone. They know they will have the support of an entire community full of persons who are only aiming to build each other up. The text does not mention a falling away of persons from the faith and yet, it supplies a method for how the church may be able to retain her emerging adult resources. This community grew day-by-day meaning that it was progressive, and so it is necessary to note that these ingredients could lead to steady improvement in the area of the attraction and retention of emerging adults. The next chapter leverages a story for church history involving the undying faith of an emerging adult and what kept her faithful until the end.

NOTES

[1] Biblical citations within the document are from the New Revised Standard Version unless otherwise noted, Second Chronicles 30:1-13, 21-27 NRSV.

[2] Dianne Bergant, *People of the Covenant: An Invitation to the Old Testament* (Franklin, WI: Sheed & Ward, 2001), 69.

[3] Adam C. Welch, *The Work of the Chronicler: Its Purpose and Its Date* (London, UK: Oxford University Press, 1939), 100.

[4] Bergant, 69.

[5] Watson E. Mills, ed., *Mercer Dictionary of the Bible* (Macon, GA: Mercer University Press, 1991), 147.

[6] Ibid.

[7] Sara Japhet, *The Ideology of the Book of Chronicles and Its Place in Biblical Thought* (Winona Lake, IN: Eisenbrauns, 2009), 3.

[8] Simon J. De Vries, *1 and 2 Chronicles, The Forms of the Old Testament Literature* (Grand Rapids, MI: William B. Eerdmans Publishing Co., 1989), 8.

[9] Jonathan Rosenbaum, "Hezekiah's Reform and the Deuteronomistic Tradition." *Harvard Theological Review* 72, no. 1-2 (January 1, 1979): 26. *ATLA Religion Database with ATLASerials*, EBSCO*host* (accessed May 19, 2013).

[10] Rosenbaum, 26.

[11] De Vries, 16.

[12] Japhet, 5.

[13] De Vries, 10.

[14] Mills, 146.

[15] Raymond B. Dillard, *2 Chronicles, World Biblical Commentary*, (Waco, TX: Word Books, 1987), 238.

[16] Steven L. McKenzie, *1-2 Chronicles, Abingdon Old Testament Commentaries* (Nashville, TN: Abingdon Press, 2004), 343.

[17] Scott W. Hahn, *The Kingdom of God as Liturgical Empire: A Theological Commentary on 1-2 Chronicles* (Grand Rapids, MI: Baker Academic Press, 2012), 177.

[18] B. Bruce Humphrey, *Ministry on Fire: Fanning the Flame of Your Congregation* (St. Louis, MO: Chalice Press, 2005), 11.

[19] Hahn, 176.

[20] Louis H. Feldman, "Josephus's Portrait of Hezekiah," *Journal Of Biblical Literature* 111, no. 4 (December 1, 1992): 604. *ATLA Religion Database with ATLASerials*, EBSCO*host* (accessed May 19, 2013).

[21] Hahn, 178.

[22] Dillard, 240.

[23] Rosenbaum, 34.

[24] Simeon Chavel, "The Second Passover, Pilgrimage, and the Centralized Cult," *Harvard Theological Review* 102, no. 1 (January 1, 2009): 7. ATLA Religion Database with ATLASerials, EBSCOhost (accessed September 3, 2014).

[25] Humphrey, 18.

[26] Ibid., 19.

[27] R. J. Coggins, *The First and Second Books of the Chronicles* (New York, NY: Cambridge University Press, 1976), 270.

[28] Dillard, 244.

[29] Japhet, 257.

[30] Hahn, 178.
[31] Ibid.
[32] Coggins, 269.
[33] Ibid., 269-270.
[34] Hahn, 178.
[35] McKenzie, 345.
[36] Hahn, 181.
[37] Ibid., 178.
[38] John Jarick, *2 Chronicles* (Sheffield, UK: Phoenix Press, 2007), 168.
[39] Rosenbaum, 34.
[40] Feldman, 604.
[41] McKenzie, 345.
[42] Feldman, 604-605.
[43] McKenzie, 345.
[44] Humphrey, 19.
[45] McKenzie, 346.
[46] Jarick, 168.
[47] Coggins, 274.
[48] Ibid., 270.
[49] Feldman, 604-605.
[50] Hahn, 177.
[51] Coggins, 274.
[52] Humphrey, 11.
[53] Humphrey, 18.
[54] Chavel, 7.
[55] Coggins, 274.
[56] Jimmy Long, *Emerging Hope: A Strategy for Reaching Postmodern Generations* (Downers Grove, IL: InterVarsity Press, 2004), 97.
[57] Pieter W. van der Horst. "Hellenistic parallels to the Acts of the Apostles 2:1-47." *Journal For The Study Of The New Testament* no. 25 (October 1, 1985): 58. ATLA Religion Database with ATLASerials, EBSCOhost (accessed February 13, 2013).

⁵⁸ David L. Tiede, "Acts 2:1-47." *Interpretation 33*, no. 1 (January 1, 1979): 66. ATLA Religion Database with ATLASerials, EBSCOhost (accessed February 13, 2013).

⁵⁹ Michael D. Coogan, *The New Oxford Annotated Bible* (New York, NY: Oxford University Press, 2007), 183.

⁶⁰ Robert W. Wall, "The Acts of the Apostles" in *Acts; Introduction to Epistolary Literature; Romans; 1 Corinthians*, vol. X of *The New Interpreter's Bible* (Nashville, TN: Abingdon Press, 2002), 5.

⁶¹ Reta Halteman Finger, "A Theology of Welcome: The Hospitable Hidden Women of Acts 2, 4, and 6." *Conrad Grebel Review 23*, no. 1 (December 1, 2005): 33. ATLA Religion Database with ATLASerials, EBSCOhost (accessed February 13, 2013).

⁶² Wall, 8

⁶³ Elwell and Beitzel, 18.

⁶⁴ John B. Polhill, *Acts* vol. 26 of The New American Commentary (Nashville, TN: Broadman & Holman Publishers, 1995), 27.

⁶⁵ Coogan, 184 New Testament

⁶⁶ John Polhill, "Acts, Book Of" in *Holman Illustrated Bible Dictionary*, ed. Chad Brand, Charles Draper, Archie England et al. (Nashville, TN: Holman Bible Publishers, 2003), 21.

⁶⁷ Finger, "A Theology of Welcome: The Hospitable Hidden Women of Acts 2, 4, and 6," 35.

⁶⁸ Ibid., 36.

⁶⁹ Ibid.

⁷⁰ Ibid., 33.

⁷¹ Polhill, *Acts*, 32.

⁷² Mills, 48.

⁷³ Polhill, *Acts*, 24-25.

⁷⁴ Mills, 49.

⁷⁵ Mark Allan Powell, "Acts of the Apostles" in *The HarperCollins Bible Dictionary*, ed. Mark Allan Powell, 3rd ed. (New York, NY: HarperCollins, 2011), 11.

⁷⁶ Wall, 12.

⁷⁷ Richard J. Dillon, "Acts of the Apostles" in *The New Jerome Biblical Commentary*, eds. Raymond E. Brown, Joseph A. Fitzmyer, and Roland E. Murphy (Old Tappan, NJ: 1990), 724-725.

[78] Gregory E. Sterling, "Athletes of Virtue" : An Analysis of the Summaries in Acts (2:41-47; 4:32-35; 5:12-16)." *Journal Of Biblical Literature* 113, no. 4 (December 1, 1994): 693. *ATLA Religion Database with ATLASerials*, EBSCO*host* (accessed March 3, 2013).
[79] Dillon, 734.
[80] Reta Halteman Finger, "Cultural Attitudes in Western Christianity toward the Community of Goods in Acts 2 and 4." *Mennonite Quarterly Review* 78, no. 2 (April 1, 2004): 238. *ATLA Religion Database with ATLASerials*, EBSCO*host* (accessed March 5, 2013).
[81] Long, 143.
[82] David P. Setran and Chris A. Kiesling, *Spiritual Formation in Emerging Adulthood: A Practical Theology for College and Young Adult Ministry* (Grand Rapids, MI: Baker Academic, 2013), 95.
[83] John E. Alsup, "Prayer, Consciousness, and the Early Church : A Look at Acts 2:41-47 for Today," *Austin Seminary Bulletin (Faculty Ed.)* 101, no. 4 (October 1, 1985): 32. *ATLA Religion Database with ATLASerials*, EBSCO*host* (accessed March 4, 2013).
[84] Dillon, 734.
[85] Ibid.
[86] Alsup, 34.
[87] Dillon, 734.
[88] Finger, "A Theology of Welcome: The Hospitable Hidden Women of Acts 2, 4, and 6," 37.
[89] Demetrius K. Williams, "The Acts of the Apostles" in *True to Our Native Land: An African American New Testament Commentary*, ed. Brian K. Blount (Minneapolis, MN: Fortress Press, 2007), 221.
[90] Pieter W. van der Horst. "Hellenistic parallels to the Acts of the Apostles 2:1-47." *Journal For The Study Of The New Testament* no. 25 (October 1, 1985): 59. *ATLA Religion Database with ATLASerials*, EBSCO*host*, accessed February 13, 2013.
[91] Ibid.
[92] Marshall, 345.
[93] Jimmy Long, *Emerging Hope: A Strategy for Reaching Postmodern Generations*, 2nd ed., (Downers Grove, IL: InterVarsity Press, 2004), 143.

[94] Alsup, 36.
[95] Alsup, 31.
[96] Finger, "A Theology of Welcome: The Hospitable Hidden Women of Acts 2, 4, and 6," 35.

CHAPTER THREE
PERPETUA'S EMERGING ADULT FAITH

Since the Bible documents the beginning of the church, it is only natural that this chapter, which arises from church history, follows. The purpose of this chapter is to establish a historical foundation by examining the Carthaginian martyr Perpetua and seek to establish ways in which a community of faith and holistic ministry helped her to develop into a young woman with such an unwavering commitment to the faith. Perpetua is regarded as the greatest of Christian heroines, according to James Halporn. The work entitled *The Passion of SS. Perpetua and Felicity* (hereafter referred to as simply *Passion*) is the means by which society is afforded the opportunity to hear Perpetua's voice and is precisely exposed to her experience, as stated by Peter Dronke. *The Passion* reported that at the time of her martyrdom Perpetua was a twenty-two year old married mother, who was virtuously born and liberally raised by her parents with her two brothers. Perpetua and her brother, according to the redactor, evidently were two catechumens in the midst of a non-Christian family had much to lose, but clung to her faith in spite of all it would cost her and those she would leave behind.

Clearly, the redactor of this work understood this passion to be ripe for "conversion and edification" so it makes sense to serve as a foundation for a ministry geared toward the retention and attraction of young adults.[1] Perpetua is an appropriate foundation for the model of ministry because of her youth and her values. Primary and secondary sources are helpful in understanding the underlying reasons for her commitment and determining what elements were necessary in order to nurture such a committed faith; such a faith which is absent from the young adults in the many churches. This chapter will focus on Perpetua's context—specifically that of the Roman Empire in the North African city of Carthage around the turn of the third century C.E.—before addressing Perpetua's community, martyrdom and the lasting effect of her martyrdom. Each of these will be presented and viewed through the lens of the model of ministry.

Perpetua's Contextual Community

Perpetua was a member of a Christian community in the city of Carthage that was part of the Roman Empire. The possibility exists that she along with others was converted during some assembly as "conversions most likely took place at the service during which Christians assembled."[2] This supports an argument that in order to retain and attract young adults to discipleship young adult Christians should invite these persons to the church where Christians assemble. However, based on observation many young adults do not often invite others to worship with them. In Perpetua's time, "strong Christian communities were important in preserving the religion and supporting the converts."[3] The "visible presence of the Spirit" is perhaps a large part of the reason that "Perpetua and many like her were persuaded to convert to Christianity."[4] This community "did not want members who were not fully committed to the total change in life that conversion implied."[5] Similarly, the model ministry should be most successful if committed members constituted the majority of its membership, but the majority of the young adults in the expected church of model implementation lack such commitment.

Perpetua was among a group of catechumens who were executed along with their teacher Saturus after being "arrested during the first years of the Severan persecutions."[6] In fact, "the edict of Severus was aimed, it seems, not at families already Christian, but against new converts from paganism" suggesting that the aim was to prevent the spread and growth of the religion.[7] Severus targeted those who possessed young faith—persons who could be more likely to cause the faith to grow through their zeal. This is perhaps one of the reasons why churches do not possess a large contingent of young adults, as majority of young adults does not have a zeal and lack charisma. Perpetua was one of these persons who were condemned while still new to the faith. Some within the Roman Empire viewed Christians as "potentially the most dangerous" opposition group and were not held in high regard by persons such as Celsus.[8] In fact, most people living at the time of Perpetua's martyrdom would have regarded her defiance of authorities and putting herself in the position to expect "torture and condemnation to the beasts" as "indefensible folly."[9] Therefore, those within her Roman Empire context misunderstood her faith in a way similar to how persons today misunderstand the Christian faith of young adults. In conversations with the young adults in my context it is clear that among their peers they feel as if their faith is misunderstood. Fortunately for Perpetua, her community supported her faith and the faith of others.

To Sullivan, *The Passion* typifies the struggle between "members of a Christian community growing increasingly self-aware and the secular Roman world"—a struggle "between realities, placing resistance into both spiritual and worldly, that is historical (sociopolitical) contexts."[10] Young adults specifically live at a critical juncture where this struggle is evident each and every day. Young adults within the church of model implementation have the same struggle. That a person of such faith could endure in the midst of an environment so similar with today's context further shows that Perpetua's experience and values undergird the model of ministry.

According to one scholar Perpetua "lived in Carthage in North Africa, where by this time there was a strong Christian community."[11] Pettersen adds that *The Passion* speaks of "the spirit of martyrdom which was then so strong in the spirituality of the hard pressed church of North Africa."[12] Perpetua was not the only person in her North African context to be committed to the extent that she was willing to die to be a witness. This is one of the benefits which Perpetua enjoys, but evades the young persons in many churches. These young adults do not have many persons around them within the same church who possess an unwavering commitment to the faith. In the absence of such support the requirement for a strong small community becomes paramount. In the words of Frend, "fear and hatred were the dominant emotions of the crowds whether at Lyon or Carthage at this time."[13] This means that not only did persons misunderstand Perpetua and her peers within the larger Roman Empire, but persons hated and feared these persons as well. At the same time, "in Carthage, the confessors were regarded as perpetrators of black magic who would be able to use their arts to escape justice."[14] Perpetua once again serves as a positive role model for the young adults of this time because she remained faithful even as persons hated her and feared her.

Reading novels in her Hellenistic world would also have influenced her perspective as "the fiction adventure stories may have helped Perpetua imagine herself as an active young woman who could withstand trials in the expectation of a happy and spiritual ending."[15] Communicating these things, which no doubt aided in her development of a positive self-image, likely would cause young adults in the contemporary to be committed in the same way as Perpetua. At the time of Tertullian, "Perpetua's contemporary and confrère,"[16] it is true that "Christianity was a subversive movement and the social change as described by Cyprian would be sufficient in itself to deter any who did not desire authentic conversion."[17] This means that this attracted persons of sincere faith, and that Perpetua was likely surrounded only with other believers who were serious in their commitment to the faith. Therefore, the model ministry should facilitate this sort of environment in a context where it seems that this sort of serious commitment among the emerging adults is absent. Such committed persons were then welcomed as catechumen in Perpetua's North African context just as Perpetua was portrayed.

From Ad Quirinum one may observe that "fundamental in the African catechetical programme was the supply of an interpretative framework for the reading of Scripture and the inculcation of the understanding of the role of a Christian in the church (though a role is not given at this stage.)"[18] Perpetua benefited from such instruction and it no doubt contributed to her unwavering commitment. Along the same lines, young adults in churches require a contemporary hermeneutic with which they may interpret scripture in light of, for example, scientific discovery. This hermeneutic would keep them from continuing to feel as if they must choose between science and faith. Also assisting them in their comprehension of the role of a Christian in the church would give them a sense of purpose, which is also missing among the several young adults in many churches.

In the words of Stewart-Sykes, "Finn attributes the survival of Christianity to the catechumenate, which he sees as a preparation for a liminal life as a Christian by enabling the candidate to recognize his or her liminal status in the world."[19] She was taught her place in the world and prepared for a life of limitations. This is what is necessary for the young adults in the church because they live in a society that seems to cast off restraints. Teaching is necessary in order for Christianity especially among young adults to survive as evidenced by Christian young adult retention and attraction. Perpetua joined a community that included Saturus, Felicity and other future martyrs. She was blessed to be in the company of Saturus whose faith was so great that he spent his last breaths ministering to the adjutant Pudens and encouraging him to "remember the faith and [him]."[20] This great man of faith "had been the person who had instructed the catechumens in the Christian faith and, therefore, must be considered their "catechist."[21] This means that she benefited from the teaching of someone who was strong in the faith. In order for persons in the target demographic of this ministry model to have a strong commitment as Perpetua did, they would need someone of faith to teach them.

In addition, as a result of the catechetical program "the formation of relationships within a tight community…was almost inevitable."[22] For Perpetua's community "there's an intense sense of community that binds together these people who are insisting on being martyred" so much so that "they take care of each other" as in the case where Perpetua and Felicity adjust each other's clothes before saying goodbye to each other.[23] Put another way, Augustine once wrote, "these martyrs…were companions together."[24] Perpetua no doubt benefited from being part of such a committed community. Young adults in today's context, while seeming to be self-absorbed in many churches, would also benefit from being surrounded with other persons of sincere faith who could encourage them and look after them in the spirit of togetherness.

Perpetua's Passion

One can learn much about Perpetua and her community of faith by studying *The Passion,* which scholars almost universally agree to be the "finest example of the genre, Acts or Lives of the Saints."[25] To

Klawiter, *The Passion* "was authored by a member of the New Prophecy, and Perpetua and Saturus stand forth as noble martyrs in that movement."[26] Regardless of the identity of the redactor who wrote the material in *The Passion* outside of the diaries of Perpetua and Saturus, the purpose outlined by the redactor for the recording or the compilation of *The Passion* is that it is to glorify God and strengthen humankind.[27] In other words, the redactor deemed that the sharing of these stories of Christian faith, trial and ultimate triumph of Perpetua and her fellow martyrs to be beneficial for Christians within a group to share with each other about their trials, tribulations and victories over temptation. In the words of Pettersen *The Passion* "reflects that Christ-like attitude of self-discipline which can render a life characterised by severe conflict and tragedy a revelation, not of hopelessness, nor of optimism despite the tragedy, but of an hope which is to be uncovered in tragedy, and to be realised de profundis."[28] Perpetua is a model of how young adults can survive all of the difficulties of life that have apprehended a hope rooted in Perpetua's savior. *The Passion* is a work that shows young adults how their faith can endure such circumstances as did Perpetua's faith.

Much of her diary centers on her dealings with her father. Perpetua remained persistent in spite of the repeated attempts of her father to "cast down [her] faith."[29] Augustine viewed her father as being used by the enemy to confront her with "words of deceit."[30] Perpetua stated that only her father would not rejoice at her passion out of all of her family.[31] This means that in spite of her father's lack of support, she had the support of the rest of her family. Such a nurturing and helpful support system likely aided in her clinging to her faith. This model of ministry should seek to accomplish the same goal in giving these persons what they currently lack in their current context—a sense of belonging and surroundings filled with persons who share the same values and who strive for similar Christian success.

Perpetua's father put her in the position to have to choose, in effect, between him and her faith.[32] The threat of family or friends becoming alienated due to one's faith is a real threat, which confronts emerging adults. It seems like a natural reaction that some will distance themselves from those of the Christian faith causing relationships to be strained or even destroyed due to a person's faith. Similarly to Perpetua, young Christian adults need to possess the same sense of ownership of their Christian identity and a persistent defiance against renouncing their Christian identification.[33] The young adults in churches currently lack such persistence and resolve. In her determination, Perpetua further serves as a foundation for the model ministry because Christian pride needs to be engendered within these young adults who lack such pride in the setting for model implementation, and who may constantly face an onslaught of persons seeking to undermine their faith or seeking to persuade them to recant their faith.

Perpetua refused to allow society to limit her identity and instead "backed by the collective identity of the Christian community" Perpetua obtained the "power to turn traditional roles upside down and to force her will upon such figures of the dominant authority as the provincial governor and her father."[34] In this vein, "by her own admission, he regards her *iam nonfiliam . . . sed dominant,* 'no longer a daughter but a mistress' (i.e., an adult woman), perhaps even a goddess. But to no avail. Neither the authority of the father nor the claim of the male child can deter Perpetua from her confession."[35] At the same time, "her diary shows a glimpse of her struggle between her duty to her infant and her duty to her faith."[36] She did not allow her obligation to her father or child to encumber her faith. Perpetua embodied how to hold on to one's faith even when it felt like one's faith conflicted with one's relationships. Young adults in churches face the same type of conflict where persons often make them choose between their faith and relationships. Surely if Perpetua could remain faithful in spite of the agony she felt in pulling away from these relationships, then the young adults which are the target of this model can do the same by following her example.

However, not every visit that Perpetua received was of an adversarial nature. While imprisoned, two deacons ministered to Perpetua and her fellow prisoners, and arranged for better living conditions.[37] This demonstrates the need for Christians, particularly young adult Christians, to receive ministration from other Christians who can help them endure and be encouraged. Unfortunately, it does not appear that this is currently the practice of the young adults in many churches based on my experience. Along the same lines, this act of arranging for better living conditions should inspire other Christians to do what they can to improve the quality of life of their brothers and sisters in the faith. Not only this, but Perpetua strengthened her brother showing that persons of faith can also benefit from the actions of other Christians while they are yet experiencing trial.[38] The young adults targeted by this model need to abandon their tunnel vision with regard to their own problems in order to be able to encourage others while going through trials themselves.

In addition to visitors, visions also played a large role in her experience while imprisoned awaiting execution. First there was her vision of her deceased brother Dinocrates. Her visions of her deceased brother and her understanding that she was in a position to help abate his punishment and her belief that her actions were heard and rewarded in the deliverance of her brother further demonstrated this ethic of looking out for others because of a sincere feeling that one can make a difference to those with whom one is connected.[39] While scholars still debate the existence of purgatory, what is evident is that Perpetua believed that it was her duty to help her brother Dinocrates from even beyond the grave by praying fervently for him in intercession.[40] Two things about this should be noted. The first is that

Perpetua shows the value of intercessory prayer from her conviction that her prayer resulted in her brother's release from purgatory.[41] Young adults need persons to pray for them that know what they are going through. The other is that this terminal sense of duty to those she loved seemed very important to her. Young people need to learn this sense of peer responsibility. This sense of peer responsibility and intercessory prayer is currently absent from the context in question.

Along with Perpetua's vision of her brother, she also experienced a detailed vision about her fate. At the beginning of section four, Perpetua reported of her agreement to ask for a vision and convey its meaning after a conversation with her brother where he encouraged her to ask for a vision that would provide clarification on the ultimate end of their ordeal.[42] She must have understood that communication with and from God was important and so must persons today from age eighteen to thirty. Many persons within this age group find themselves seeking answers, wisdom and guidance, including in the context in question, and here they can understand from Perpetua that seeking God will pay off. Perpetua was granted a vision in response to her request.[43] One of the first things she saw in the vision was a bronze ladder,[44] and Augustine believed that this "upward ladder was shown her whereby she should go to God."[45] All along the ladder were "weapons of war and torture" that "threatened to mangle the flesh of the careless climber."[46] To Perpetua, young Christians should expect to suffer on their way to heaven, and they should understand that they will face opposition with the intent of the keeping them from remaining faithful. Perpetua demonstrated the resolve to be faithful no matter the cost and young Christians benefit from such an example. Next she saw a serpent at the foot of the ladder,[47] and Augustine wrote that Perpetua viewed the serpent was a "stone of stumbling."[48] The vision seemed to convey that she would be able to overcome any obstacle to her reaching God and receiving her reward.

Lastly, Perpetua experienced one last vision where she envisioned herself transforming into a man.[49] It suggests, "Perpetua is a positive example of women's empowerment in the early church" as "this empowerment was usually expressed, in the Jewish and Christian tradition, in terms of these women becoming 'like a man.'"[50] This shows that she had a healthy self-image and a proper sense of self-worth. She did not see herself as being too weak to weather the trails—in spite of her gender she felt equipped to endure. The model ministry should encourage this sense of healthy self-image if it is to attract and retain emerging adults.

Halporn noted, "they suffered martyrdom on 7 March, as part of the festivities celebrating the birthday of the Caesar, Geta, the son of the reigning emperor, Septimius Severus."[51] On several occasions Perpetua demonstrated the type of courage of faith that is lacking in the young adults in some churches. One of these times included when she began to sing just before heading to the amphitheater.[52] The prospect of martyrdom engendered a sense of fearlessness among the faithful and a rejoicing at the prospect of suffering with Christ.[53] Klawiter noted that *The Passion* provides "an eloquent and moving testimony to the power and courage of the noble martyrs."[54] Perpetua remains an inspiration due to the courage and power with which she suffered while clinging to an unshakeable faith. Her example also shows that in order for young adults to have the same type of commitment they need to be surrounded with other persons who are courageous in facing the costs of Christian discipleship. She showed courage and the Montanist characteristic of leadership in rebuking the military tribune about the poor treatment of Perpetua and her fellow prisoners by speaking to him directly.[55] The target context is a place where its young people largely walk around without confidence and lack the skill of clear direct communication. Perpetua provided a lesson on the importance of standing up for oneself as well as raising ones voice in intercession for others. The conviction of receiving a reward was part of what kept Perpetua faithful.[56] The model ministry must keep the big picture in the minds and hearts of young adults so that they may connect their present suffering and struggle with future reward.

When directed to put on the dress of the priestesses of Ceres, Perpetua refused, thereby, demonstrating her refusal to conform and identify with pagans in the process.[57] Teaching young people about the dangers of conformity is important. At a time when they may feel more pressure to conform, Perpetua teaches them that standing apart for the cause of Christ is something to be commended and valued by young adults. She shows that it is possible to remain faithful to one's Christian faith as a young adult without compromising with worldly standards. As a result an effective ministry to young adults ages eighteen to thirty would have to encourage this given the dialectic such persons would feel between being faithful Christians and a part of the emerging adulthood. Clothed in a loose robe, when Perpetua was thrown and "fell upon her loins," she sat up and pulled her torn robe to cover her thigh because she was "mindful rather of modesty than of pain."[58] She then searched for a pin for the purpose of pinning up "her dishevelled hair; for it was not meet that a martyr should suffer with hair dishevelled, lest she should seem to grieve in her glory."[59] She was more concerned about integrity and dignity or more concerned about the effect of her immodesty on the kingdom than of her personal suffering. Instead of being self-absorbed, Perpetua was selfless again modeling the necessary values for the emerging adults in churches.

There was no discord in Perpetua and Felicity who participated in various activities such as singing, dying, and battling "against the maddened cow" together.[60] When she saw Felicity knocked down, she approached her and helped her to her feet, and in the words of the redactor they "stood up together."[61] This means helping each other up to stand on their feet even when suffering themselves. None of us lives within a vacuum and so emerging adults need to know how and prepared to assist others even when they are at less than full strength. This incident, called "a very affecting scene," demonstrated what Fredriksen referred to as "an intense sense of community that binds together these people who are insisting on being martyred" where "they take care of each other."[62] In this act, they demonstrate once again the importance of community. Before the end came, "they say good-bye to each other in this life with the kiss of peace" as a further testament of their togetherness and unity.[63]

After awaking from a sort of trance, she encouraged her brother and his fellow catechumen to "stand fast in the faith, and love ye all one another."[64] She also asked them to not allow the trial these martyrs endured to weaken them[65] or cause them to "fall into unbelief."[66] These facts further demonstrate a willingness on her part to encourage others even from her pain. Personal suffering is not an excuse to be apathetic toward encouraging others or giving others what they need. In a period where emerging adults may feel even more isolated, they need the encouragement of others who occupy the same space. Perpetua set the blade of the swordsman up to her own neck as the redactor wrote "perchance so great a woman could not else have been slain (being feared of the unclean spirit) had she not herself so willed it."[67] Once again Perpetua's courage and conviction was on display serving as a paradigm for young adults who need to have the courage of their convictions. This woman of unshakeable faith "freely accepted the situation in which she was, allowing it to test her faith in God, to confirm the unshakable faithfulness of God towards her and to condemn the false assumptions of religiosity."[68] In other words, she understood that her trial was a challenge to her loyalty to God, but designed to affirm God's loyalty to her. Young adults need to have Perpetua's perspective on trials so that they do not lose sight of the larger picture.

Aftermath

The effects of Perpetua's life and death were felt across the region and the people commemorated her courage in several ways. For example, the Basilica Marjoram commemorated the martyrdom.[69] Along these lines, "the details of the arrest, imprisonment, trial, and execution of Perpetua and her companions were kept alive (and expanded upon) in the memory of the North-African Christian communities through the public reading of the various editions" of *The Passion* and Acta in the liturgy of their "feast days."[70] Also, "they were regarded as saints; the date of their martyrdom was celebrated… and sermons commemorating them were preached by no less an authority than Augustine."[71] This showed that incentive exists for young adults to exemplify Christian character for their example can affect persons that come generations after them. Some young people seem to lack a sense of purpose, but Perpetua and her friends showed that part of the Christian's purpose is to make an impact on the world and to encourage their descendants by leading lives of integrity.

With regard to her impact around the time of her death, at least one person became a Christian. Perpetua reported at Pudens the adjutant of the prison "understood that there was much grace in [them]"[72] before then believing in the gospel before the martyrdom of Perpetua and her friends.[73] In other words, through his encounter with these Christian prisoners he came to believe in the same faith that gave them peace in spite of facing death as the ultimate witness for Christ. A ministry that promotes Christian confidence and assurance would no doubt draw others to the faith in the same manner as Perpetua and her friends. Along the same lines, many others believed after the proclamation of judgments by the martyrs, including Saturus, during a celebration of the Agape or Love Feast.[74] Facing the ultimate of trail and tribulation did not deter these persons from using some of their final moments to preach the gospel. Lifestyle is a more effective sermon. They were in this together, while Saturus is singled out as one who spoke the text reported, "they cast these words at the people."[75] Her story equips the church with an evangelistic model based on living one's life with integrity, but also using the best words at the most effective of times—being authentic when it counts the most or when given every incentive, including death, to abandon one's faith.

When it came to later impacts across North Africa, "the early history of North African Christianity was decisively shaped by these and other experiences of martyrdom."[76] Many of the new converts in Carthage "no doubt were inspired by the example of the martyrs."[77] This means that their faithfulness and unwavering commitment inspired others and assisted in the growth of the Christian community. One could attach significance to the fact that "even as late as the fifth century, Perpetua was remembered as a martyr in both the catholic and Montanist communities of North Africa," and likely "the persecution of 203 happened when the New Prophecy had not yet been rejected by the Carthaginian catholic community."[78] *The Passion* itself "was a direct source of inspiration for two North African passions" due to its position of authority in North African Christian circles as evidenced by its use in liturgy."[79] The events reported in the Acta "was to serve the community as an edifying example of the rejection of worldly ties for the sake of the community of Christians."[80] It appears that Perpetua, "given the language and imagery… was seen as a role model for other Christians."[81] Emerging adults need role models and need to serve as examples to their peers and to others.

One of the things that made this feat for Perpetua even more impressive to persons in antiquity is that women were generally considered to be the weaker gender as evidenced by Augustine's reference to them as being members of the gender "more frail" and having "womanly weakness."[82] Perpetua, therefore, likely remains an inspiration for young women of faith. If she could overcome all of these challenges as a young woman surely emerging adults in the church can do the same. Perpetua's "willingness to die is not only an act of faith and maturity, but in existential terms, a political act against her environment" demonstrating that "in seeking martyrdom she was as much concerned with solving problems in this life as with attaining perfection in the next."[83] This means that she was concerned with more than just spiritual matters and sought to have a greater impact. This reflects the psyche of emerging adults with whom I have conversed who want answers to their problems on this side and for whom faith has to answer issues raised in this life. The hope is the same for this ministry—that it would affect the whole person and inspire them to avoid having a narrow theology in which only spiritual matters are discussed.

Conclusion

Augustine once proclaimed to a congregation regarding the actions of Perpetua, Felicity and the other martyrs and how they have shown Christians the way stating that "they have gone before us, they have shown out before us. If we may not follow them in deeds, let us follow them in affection…if not in eminence, in communion."[84] One may interpret these words to mean that Christians should follow their example and thereby providing support for the idea that Perpetua's example serves as sufficient example for Christians in general and young adults in particular. Perpetua's life and death served not only as an inspiration for people of faith during her time, but they provide hope for the Christian young adults of today. Her example should impact all Christian believers, especially emerging adults as she was at the time of her martyrdom. In examining both primary and secondary sources, this chapter has shown how Perpetua's life and death provide a foundational model for the model ministry to emerging adults. Using her example, it is possible to build a holistic ministry for young adults that will engender a strong commitment to the Christian faith. This ministry, with Perpetua as a paradigm, can also serve as a catalyst for the retention and attraction of more Christian young adults. As she has shown, youth is not adversarial to Christian commitment; instead with youth comes the prospect of exchanging the old ways for a better way forward. Next, the book turns its attention to systematic theology and how one particular branch supports the inclusion of community as an important factor in attracting and retaining emerging adults.

NOTES

[1] Gail P. C. Streete, *Redeemed Bodies: Women Martyrs in Early Christianity* (Louisville, KY: Westminster John Knox Press, 2009), 49.

[2] Joyce E. Salisbury, *Perpetua's Passion: The Death and Memory of a Young Roman Woman* (New York, NY: Routledge, 1997), 62.

[3] Ibid.

[4] Ibid, 71.

[5] Ibid, 73.

[6] James W. Halporn, *Passio Sanctarum: Perpetuae et Felicitatis*, Bryn Mawr Latin Commentaries, ed. Julia Haig Gaisser and James J. O'Donnell (Bryn Mawr, PA: Bryn Mawr College, 1984), 3-4.

[7] Augustine and Walter Shewring, *The Passion of SS. Perpetua and Felicity, MM: A New Edition and Translation of the Latin Text, Together with the Sermons of St. Augustine Upon These Saints, Now First Translated into English* (London, UK: Sheed and Ward, 1931), xiii.

[8] William H. C. Frend, "Blandina and Perpetua: Two Early Christian Heroines" in *Women in Early Christianity*, vol. XIV of Studies in Earlier Christianity, ed. David M. Scholer (New York, NY: Garland Publishing, Inc., 1993), 88-89.

[9] Ibid., 87.

[10] Lisa M. Sullivan, "I Responded, 'I Will Not...'" : Christianity as Catalyst for Resistance in the Passio Perpetuae et Felicitatis." *Semeia* no. 79 (January 1, 1997): 63. *ATLA Religion Database with ATLASerials*, EBSCO*host* (accessed March 6, 2013).

[11] David M. Scholer, "And I was a Man" : The Power and Problem of Perpetua," *Daughters Of Sarah* 15, no. 5 (September 1, 1989): 10.

ATLA Religion Database with ATLASerials, EBSCO*host* (accessed March 6, 2013).

[12] Alvyn Pettersen, "Perpetua - Prisoner of Conscience," *Vigiliae Christianae* 41, no. 2 (June 1, 1987): 139. *ATLA Religion Database with ATLASerials*, EBSCO*host* (accessed March 6, 2013).

[13] William H. C. Frend, "Blandina and Perpetua: Two Early Christian Heroines" in *Women in Early Christianity*, vol. XIV of Studies in Earlier Christianity, ed. David M. Scholer (New York, NY: Garland Publishing, Inc., 1993), 87.

[14] Ibid.

[15] Joyce E. Salisbury, *Perpetua's Passion: The Death and Memory of a Young Roman Woman* (New York, NY: Routledge, 1997), 49.

[16] Patricia Cox Miller, "A Dubious Twilight" : Reflections on Dreams in Patristic Literature," *Church History* 55, no. 2 (June 1, 1986): 157. *ATLA Religion Database with ATLASerials*, EBSCO*host* (accessed March 6, 2013).

[17] Alistair Stewart-Sykes, "Catechumenate and Contra-Culture: The Social Process of Catechumenate in Third-Century Africa and its Development," *St Vladimir's Theological Quarterly* 47, no. 3-4 (January 1, 2003): 299. *ATLA Religion Database with ATLASerials*, EBSCO*host* (accessed March 6, 2013).

[18] Ibid., 300.

[19] Ibid., 301.

[20] Augustine and Walter Shewring, *The Passion of SS. Perpetua and Felicity, MM: A New Edition and Translation of the Latin Text, Together with the Sermons of St. Augustine Upon These Saints, Now First Translated into English* (London, UK: Sheed and Ward, 1931), 41.

[21] William Tabbernee, "Perpetua, Montanism, and Christian Ministry in Carthage c. 203 C.E." *Perspectives In Religious Studies* 32, no. 4 (December 1, 2005): 432-433. *ATLA Religion Database with ATLASerials*, EBSCO*host* (accessed March 6, 2013).

[22] Alistair Stewart-Sykes, "Catechumenate and Contra-Culture: The Social Process of Catechumenate in Third-Century Africa and its Development." *St Vladimir's Theological Quarterly* 47, no. 3-4 (January 1, 2003): 300. *ATLA Religion Database with ATLASerials*, EBSCO*host* (accessed March 6, 2013).

[23] Paula Fredriksen, under "THE MARTYRDOM OF PERPETUA," accessed March 7, 2013, http://www.pbs.org/wgbh/pages/frontline/shows/religion/why/martyrs.html.

[24] Augustine and Walter Shewring, *The Passion of SS. Perpetua and Felicity, MM: A New Edition and Translation of the Latin Text, Together with the Sermons of St. Augustine Upon These Saints, Now First Translated into English* (London, UK: Sheed and Ward, 1931), 52.

[25] James W. Halporn, *Passio Sanctarum: Perpetuae et Felicitatis*, Bryn Mawr Latin Commentaries, ed. Julia Haig Gaisser and James J. O'Donnell (Bryn Mawr, PA: Bryn Mawr College, 1984), 3.

[26] Frederick C. Klawiter, "The Role of Martyrdom and Persecution in Developing the Priestly Authority of Women in Early Christianity : A Case Study of Montanism," *Church History* 49, no. 3 (September 1, 1980): 257. *ATLA Religion Database with ATLASerials*, EBSCO*host* (accessed March 6, 2013).

[27] C.f. Augustine and Walter Shewring, *The Passion of SS. Perpetua and Felicity, MM: A New Edition and Translation of the Latin Text, Together with the Sermons of St. Augustine Upon These Saints, Now First Translated into English* (London, UK: Sheed and Ward, 1931), 22.

[28] Alvyn Pettersen, "Perpetua - Prisoner of Conscience," *Vigiliae Christianae* 41, no. 2 (June 1, 1987): 149. *ATLA Religion Database with ATLASerials*, EBSCO*host* (accessed March 6, 2013).

[29] Augustine and Walter Shewring, *The Passion of SS. Perpetua and Felicity, MM: A New Edition and Translation of the Latin Text, Together with the Sermons of St. Augustine Upon These Saints, Now First Translated into English* (London, UK: Sheed and Ward, 1931), 27.

[30] Ibid., 53.
[31] Ibid., 27.
[32] Ibid., 24.
[33] C.f. Ibid., 24.
[34] Lisa M. Sullivan, "I Responded, 'I Will Not...'" : Christianity as Catalyst for Resistance in the Passio Perpetuae et Felicitatis." *Semeia*

no. 79 (January 1, 1997): 73. *ATLA Religion Database with ATLASerials*, EBSCO*host* (accessed March 6, 2013).

[35] Francine Cardman, "Acts of the Women Martyrs," *Anglican Theological Review* 70, no. 2 (April 1, 1988): 147. *ATLA Religion Database with ATLASerials*, EBSCO*host* (accessed March 6, 2013).

[36] William H. C. Frend, "Blandina and Perpetua: Two Early Christian Heroines" in *Women in Early Christianity*, vol. XIV of Studies in Earlier Christianity, ed. David M. Scholer (New York, NY: Garland Publishing, Inc., 1993), 90.

[37] Augustine and Walter Shewring, *The Passion of SS. Perpetua and Felicity, MM: A New Edition and Translation of the Latin Text, Together with the Sermons of St. Augustine Upon These Saints, Now First Translated into English* (London, UK: Sheed and Ward, 1931), 25.

[38] Ibid.

[39] C.f. Ibid., 28-30.

[40] Ibid.

[41] Ibid., 30.

[42] Ibid., 25.

[43] Ibid.

[44] Ibid.

[45] Ibid, 46.

[46] Rex D. Butler, The New Prophecy and "New Visions," vol. 18 of North American Patristic Society Patristic Monograph Series, ed. Philip Rousseau (Washington, D.C.: The Catholic University of America Press, 2006), 64.

[47] Augustine and Walter Shewring, *The Passion of SS. Perpetua and Felicity, MM: A New Edition and Translation of the Latin Text, Together with the Sermons of St. Augustine Upon These Saints, Now First Translated into English* (London, UK: Sheed and Ward, 1931), 26.

[48] Ibid., 46.

[49] Ibid., 23.

[50] David M. Scholer, "And I was a Man" : The Power and Problem of Perpetua," Daughters Of Sarah 15, no. 5 (September 1, 1989): 14. ATLA Religion Database with ATLASerials, EBSCOhost (accessed March 6, 2013).

⁵¹ James W. Halporn, "Literary History and Generic Expectations in the Passio and Acta Perpetuae," *Vigiliae Christianae* 45, no. 3 (September 1, 1991): 225. *ATLA Religion Database with ATLASerials*, EBSCO*host* (accessed March 6, 2013).

⁵² Augustine and Walter Shewring, *The Passion of SS. Perpetua and Felicity, MM: A New Edition and Translation of the Latin Text, Together with the Sermons of St. Augustine Upon These Saints, Now First Translated into English* (London, UK: Sheed and Ward, 1931), 38.

⁵³ C.f. Ibid., 37.

⁵⁴ Frederick C. Klawiter, "The Role of Martyrdom and Persecution in Developing the Priestly Authority of Women in Early Christianity : A Case Study of Montanism," *Church History* 49, no. 3 (September 1, 1980): 257. *ATLA Religion Database with ATLASerials*, EBSCO*host* (accessed March 6, 2013).

⁵⁵ Rex D. Butler, The New Prophecy & "New Visions", vol. 18 of North American Patristic Society Patristic Monograph Series, ed. Philip Rousseau (Washington, D.C.: The Catholic University of America Press, 2006), 85.

⁵⁶ C.f. Augustine and Walter Shewring, *The Passion of SS. Perpetua and Felicity, MM: A New Edition and Translation of the Latin Text, Together with the Sermons of St. Augustine Upon These Saints, Now First Translated into English* (London, UK: Sheed and Ward, 1931), 34.

⁵⁷ Ibid., 38.
⁵⁸ Ibid., 40.
⁵⁹ Ibid.
⁶⁰ Ibid., 57.
⁶¹ Ibid., 40.
⁶² Paula Fredriksen, under "THE MARTYRDOM OF PERPETUA," accessed March 7, 2013, http://www.pbs.org/wgbh/pages/frontline/shows/religion/why/martyrs.html.
⁶³ Ibid.
⁶⁴ Augustine and Walter Shewring, *The Passion of SS. Perpetua and Felicity, MM: A New Edition and Translation of the Latin Text, Together with the Sermons of St. Augustine Upon These Saints, Now*

First Translated into English (London, UK: Sheed and Ward, 1931), 40.

[65] William H. C. Frend, "Blandina and Perpetua: Two Early Christian Heroines" in *Women in Early Christianity*, vol. XIV of Studies in Earlier Christianity, ed. David M. Scholer (New York, NY: Garland Publishing, Inc., 1993), 91.

[66] James W. Halporn, *Passio Sanctarum: Perpetuae et Felicitatis*, Bryn Mawr Latin Commentaries, ed. Julia Haig Gaisser and James J. O'Donnell (Bryn Mawr, PA: Bryn Mawr College, 1984), 55.

[67] Augustine and Walter Shewring, *The Passion of SS. Perpetua and Felicity, MM: A New Edition and Translation of the Latin Text, Together with the Sermons of St. Augustine Upon These Saints, Now First Translated into English* (London, UK: Sheed and Ward, 1931), 42.

[68] Alvyn Pettersen, "Perpetua - Prisoner of Conscience." *Vigiliae Christianae* 41, no. 2 (June 1, 1987): 141. *ATLA Religion Database with ATLASerials*, EBSCO*host* (accessed March 6, 2013).

[69] Paul MacKendrick, "From the Military Anarchy to the Arab Invasion" in *The North African Stones Speak*, (Chapel Hill, NC: University of North Carolina Press, 1980), 99.

[70] William Tabbernee, "Perpetua, Montanism, and Christian Ministry in Carthage c. 203 C.E." *Perspectives In Religious Studies* 32, no. 4 (December 1, 2005): 424. *ATLA Religion Database with ATLASerials*, EBSCO*host* (accessed March 6, 2013).

[71] Rex D. Butler, The New Prophecy and "New Visions," vol. 18 of North American Patristic Society Patristic Monograph Series, ed. Philip Rousseau (Washington, D.C.: The Catholic University of America Press, 2006), 97.

[72] Augustine and Walter Shewring, *The Passion of SS. Perpetua and Felicity, MM: A New Edition and Translation of the Latin Text, Together with the Sermons of St. Augustine Upon These Saints, Now First Translated into English* (London, UK: Sheed and Ward, 1931), 30.

[73] Ibid., 37.

[74] Ibid.

[75] Ibid.

[76] Dale T. Irvin and Scott W. Sunquist, *History of the World Christian Movement* (Maryknoll, NY: Orbis Books, 2001), 83.

⁷⁷ Joyce E. Salisbury, *Perpetua's Passion: The Death and Memory of a Young Roman Woman* (New York, NY: Routledge, 1997), 156.

⁷⁸ Frederick C. Klawiter, "The Role of Martyrdom and Persecution in Developing the Priestly Authority of Women in Early Christianity : A Case Study of Montanism," *Church History* 49, no. 3 (September 1, 1980): 257. *ATLA Religion Database with ATLASerials*, EBSCO*host* (accessed March 6, 2013).

⁷⁹ Jaakko Aronen, "Indebtedness to Passio Perpetuae in Pontius' Vita Cypriani." *Vigiliae Christianae* 38, no. 1 (March 1, 1984): 67. *ATLA Religion Database with ATLASerials*, EBSCO*host* (accessed March 6, 2013).

⁸⁰ James W. Halporn, "Literary History and Generic Expectations in the Passio and Acta Perpetuae," *Vigiliae Christianae* 45, no. 3 (September 1, 1991): 230. *ATLA Religion Database with ATLASerials*, EBSCO*host* (accessed March 6, 2013).

⁸¹ Lisa M. Sullivan, "I Responded, 'I Will Not...' : Christianity as Catalyst for Resistance in the Passio Perpetuae et Felicitatis." *Semeia* no. 79 (January 1, 1997): 66. *ATLA Religion Database with ATLASerials*, EBSCO*host* (accessed March 6, 2013).

⁸² Augustine and Walter Shewring, *The Passion of SS. Perpetua and Felicity, MM: A New Edition and Translation of the Latin Text, Together with the Sermons of St. Augustine Upon These Saints, Now First Translated into English* (London, UK: Sheed and Ward, 1931), 52.

⁸³ Mary R. Lefkowitz, "Motivations for St. Perpetua's Martyrdom," Journal Of The American Academy Of Religion 44, no. 3 (September 1, 1976): 421. ATLA Religion Database with ATLASerials, EBSCOhost (accessed March 6, 2013).

⁸⁴ Ibid., 51.

CHAPTER FOUR
LESSONS FROM LIBERATION THEOLOGY

Liberation theology serves as a sensible theological foundation for a model of ministry for attracting and retaining emerging adults due to its emphasis on interpreting the faith in the context of community and addressing the needs of the whole person in an effort to make the faith relevant. By focusing on delivering persons from oppression especially economic oppression, liberation theology is rooted in an ethic of the Christian community addressing the holistic needs of humankind both inside and outside the walls of the church institution. The second phase of the Enlightenment according to Jon Sobrino addressed the needs of holistic perspective, which included or permitted economic and political alienation. More recently, James Cone introduced the term theology of liberation or liberation theology while others introduced revolution theologies in the late 1960's. Additionally, liberation theology presented itself in Latin America in the 1960's as well; yet, its roots can be traced back to the work of Walter Rauschenbusch in

LESSONS FROM LIBERATION THEOLOGY 73

the 1920s in North America according to David Benner and Peter Hill. In examining the concepts of liberation theologies the struggle lies within the issues of faith and post – colonial deprivation, which searches for hope in a poverty-stricken world and asks, "'Where is the God of righteousness in a world of injustice?'"[1] as stated in the *New Dictionary of Theology* authored by Sinclair B. Ferguson and J.I. Packer. An example of a scripture that supports this hermeneutic states that, "The Spirit of the Lord is upon me, because he has anointed me to bring good news to the poor. He has sent me to proclaim release to the captives and recovery of sight to the blind, to let the oppressed go free, to proclaim the year of the Lord's favor," (Luke 4:18-19).

Often celebrated as one of the founders of liberation theology, the "Peruvian Gustavo Gutierrez's *Teología de la liberación,* published at Lima in 1971 (Eng. tr., *A Theology of Liberation,* 1974), provides an accessible introduction."[2] Gutierrez "defines saving faith in a very practical manner as 'an act of trust, a going out of one's self, a commitment to God and neighbor, a relationship with others.'"[3] Therefore, it makes sense that "sin, for Gutierrez, is the negation of one's fellow human being as a brother."[4] Gutierrez wrote, "sin is regarded as a social, historical fact, the absence of fellowship and love in relationship among persons, the breach of friendship with God and with other persons, and therefore, an interior, personal fracture."[5] Gutierrez's beliefs undergird an argument for holistic ministry and support the critical nature of relationships and community for Christians. The church of interest has room to grow in the areas of crafting a theology and practice that addresses the holistic concerns of emerging adults and that leverages community as a tool for positive faith development.

Gutierrez also wrote, "people should be emancipated from those things that limit their capacity to develop themselves."[6] In the case of churches, one of the elements that emerging adults may find limiting to their development is the insistence on tradition to the exclusion of more contemporary ministry practices. On the other hand a model built upon a foundation of liberation theology can conversely add things such as community structure in the cases where the absence of such elements hinders emerging adult holistic development. This means holding and encouraging participation in communal dialogue that addresses the arresting issues of the time such as abortion and homosexuality without fear of rejection or judgment. In reference to Gutierrez's work *We Drink from Our Own Wells: The Spiritual Journey of a People*, Horrell writes, "in part one, Gutierrez explains anew 'the contextual experience that is the matrix or crucible of the spirituality now being born in Latin America.'"[7] Put another way, experience shapes and develops theology especially when that theology seeks to make sense of conditions that seem out of step with God's intent.

Another important contributor of the movement is Leonardo Boff. One could argue that liberation theology, in part, is a making of the gospel relevant to oppressed persons by keeping the memory of Jesus' crucifixion alive; the content of this memory being liberation.[8] Since "liberation is the comprehensive backdrop against which theologians reflect on the entire content of their faith," it could be stated that it is a hermeneutical lens through which theologians examine the relevance or meaning of their faith in light of circumstances that affect the whole person.[9] To Boff, "salvation is integral; it concerns not only the spirit but the body and the world as well."[10] Put another way, integral liberation means the "liberation of the whole human being and all human beings—the liberation of all oppressed dimensions, personal and social, of human life in all of the subjects of that life, without the exclusion of anyone or anything."[11] Boff also wrote that liberation "means principally, though not exclusively, the economic, political, and social liberation of oppressed peoples."[12] He further scribed that spiritual liberation is connected to other liberations and without spiritual liberation "no other liberation would have definitive significance."[13]

Boff was correct in asserting that the "Church is the community of the faithful who come together in an awareness" of the truth of "Jesus' deed of liberation" and the fact that "all creation is penetrated by the Spirit of Jesus."[14] Truly, the "community of the faithful is signed with the seal of love, that it may be the place of understanding, of forgiveness, of communion, of new being."[15] Boff then legitimately stated, "Jesus' ideal is a society, neither of opulence nor of poverty, but a society of justice and communion among sisters and brothers."[16] At another point, Boff correctly concludes, "faith is ever the creative vehicle of a community spirit and community practices."[17] Logically, Boff would opine that the "appearance of base communities is the most important event to have occurred in the Church for centuries" because they liberated the "captive word" by giving people the floor who had long been silenced by society and the Church.[18] This hearkens back to the description of churches where the voices of emerging adults have been muted thereby necessitating a forum in which they can speak freely. These base church communities became the "locus of the appearance of a new kind of vital social community, a community of more partnership, solidarity, and participation."[19] Therefore they offer a paradigm for what is necessary in order to attract and retain emerging adults in a context that lacks partnership, solidarity, and participation among its emerging adults. Boff correctly held up these base communities because "the network of base communities has restored the larger Church to its status as a community, enabling it to root its faith in history and integrating into the mystery of the salvation of Jesus Christ the burning desires of the people for more humane living conditions."[20]

David Smith contributes valuable information to this dialogue as he offers that "liberation theology goes toward the social sciences.

'Through them theology gains a concrete understanding of the world in which faith is lived, and, therefore, of the questions which it must respond to in order to enable Christians to test and strengthen the efficacy of their obedience.'"[21] In defining liberation theology, first it becomes helpful to define liberation and theology. With this in mind, theology is the "fruit of life in community, of shared faith, and of multiple efforts (often invisible and unrecognized), and it should be acknowledged and encouraged as such, as a shared responsibility of all members of a believing, Spirit-filled human community."[22] In the case of liberation theology, "liberation is freedom from sin and communion with God and this provides the basis for true brotherhood."[23] In other words, Christianity along with its founding principles becomes the foundation for liberation theology. Gareth Icenogle alludes to a liberation theology for Jesus who "called out a small group of people to experience their own exodus together, to move from enslavement of controlling social, political and religious patterns and to enter into the freedom of 'pouring new wine into new wineskins.'"[24]

Alternatively, "[Jesus] is the one who sets man free and who enables man to live in communion and harmony with others."[25] In line with Gutierrez's definition, "to the extent that sin is selfishness, a refusal to love the neighbor, or Christ himself, it creates the breach of brotherhood. Such a disruption is the ultimate cause of the injustice, oppression, and poverty in which men live, according to the Bible."[26] Explained otherwise Jesus called persons to experience their faith journey in community and to affect the lives of others in a holistic way. This foundation for liberation theology reinforces the effectiveness of liberation theology as a foundation for the model of ministry. In what seems to be an individualized faith walk for emerging adults, returning to Jesus' community helps to bring clarity to the beneficial nature of community. Benner and Hill also add valuable insight to this discussion in writing the following:

> Liberation theology is an endeavor to interpret the message of the Christian gospel primarily in terms of social revolution in solidarity with the poor or oppressed people of society. At its center is the claim that the salvation the gospel reveals is that of deliverance of humankind from every form of institutionalized disadvantage that prevents the full actualization in every person of all those potentials for creativity, meaning, self-realization, freedom, and community with which God has endowed us in making us in his image (Gen. 1). Liberation theology urges that the task of the church in the world is to implement sociopolitical liberation of the poor, oppressed, and disadvantaged from those political, social, legal, or economic forces that reserve the power in society for the established power structures and prevent the needy from participating in shaping their own destinies. [27]

Liberation theology therefore helps persons to connect the good news of Jesus Christ with the conditions Christians experience in context rather than solely attaching the gospel to a heavenly reward. Liberation theology also provides necessary systematic theological underpinnings for addressing the issue of emerging adult attraction and retention because it utilizes a multifaceted method:

> Liberation theology employs a method whose principal source is not reason (as in natural law theology), nor tradition (as in many institutions), nor the Bible (as in evangelicalism), nor the voice of the Spirit (as in some charismatic circles), nor social analysis (as in some liberal circles), but in a Christian praxis which enlists all of the above.[28]

At the same time, "liberation theologians argue that praxis—the unity of theory and practice in a concrete historical situation—is the starting point for theology...Theology is the reflection on our experience of committed action in light of the Bible."[29] Praxis helps emerging adults by providing a platform to reflect on their efforts to live theology rather than just recite it. Conn rightly notes, "through praxis people seek not merely to understand the word but to change it."[30] Rutschman also offers "It is well to remember that Liberation Theology is a second act, the reflection on praxis in the light of the Word…in Latin American Liberation Theology, [praxis] can be described as the two-way traffic between theory and practice in a way that suggests a hermeneutical circulation between the situation and the Word."[31] Liberation theology undergirds the need for ministry to emerging adults by supporting a paradigm where they seek to make sense of the world in which they live. Put yet another way, "the ultimate stage of conscientization, for liberation theologians at least, is a communal experience of Christ the liberator apprehended in the praxis of Christian faith."[32] The component of praxis in liberation theology supports a method for attracting and retaining young adults by placing emphasis on reflection rather than simply accepting dogma or acting without thinking within authentic community.

Liberation theology consists of several themes depending on the sources one utilizes. For example, June O'Connor offers, "themes of human power, creativity, and responsibility for the future pervade liberation theology."[33] At the same time, another source adds that the themes of liberation theology include the concepts that, "God is on the side of the poor and the oppressed;" "Jesus, the supreme revelation of God, identified with the poor, denounced economic and sexual oppression, and took on the suffering of the world in order to set it free;" "authentic faith includes the practice of liberation;" the "church is called to be a prophet against social injustice;" "conflict is necessary;" "reform is not enough;" and "history is an indivisible unity."[34] Sutphin also notes that in reference to one of the themes common to various liberation theologies called "humanization."[35]

> [Letty] Russell insists that the essential factors are the need to be accepted as a subject, not as an object or thing which is always manipulated by others, the need to participate in the

shaping and understanding of the world in which the individual finds himself, and the need of a supportive community.[36]

In sum, these themes undergird the need for a theology that empowers, holds persons accountable, addresses holistic needs of others, and that emphasizes the importance of supportive community. Churches has potential for growth in each of these areas especially as a means to leading the church toward wholeness with regard to addressing emerging adult attraction and retention.

Liberation theology also supports the model of ministry because it emphasizes the addressing of the holistic needs of the oppressed. McGrath writes, "liberation theology has tended to equate salvation with liberation, and stressed the social, political, and economic aspects of salvation."[37] Leonardo Boff writes that the "salvation proclaimed by Christianity is an all-embracing one. It is not restricted to economic, political, social and ideological emancipation, but neither can it be realized without them."[38] Volf adds "whereas salvation is 'the terminal situation of the human being in God liberations are stages along the way to this terminal situation."[39] As it pertains to the model of ministry this means that there is a holistic element to salvation that suggests that the holistic concerns of humanity need to be addressed in ministry including ministry tailored to emerging adults. Each part affects the whole and so a ministry that will be relevant to emerging adults needs not only to address spiritual concerns, but also provide safe space and authentic community for dialogue surrounding the issues that affect everyday life. This is because David Tracy correctly states, "Christian salvation is not exhausted by any program of political liberation, to be sure, but Christian salvation, rightly understood, cannot be divorced from the struggle for total human liberation—individual, social, political, and religious."[40] A ministry that fails to discuss the difficulties within context of emerging adults and fails to, as Sutphin suggests, deal with their "hopes, needs, and concerns" of a holistic nature fails to impress upon emerging adults the relevance of the church to their lives.[41]

When connected with the issue of praxis, it therefore becomes sensible to recognize that "liberation theology is committed to the work of transforming this world, this history, since salvation embraces all men and the whole man."[42] Another source offers with regard to liberation theologians that the "salient features of their thought are: (1) a preferential option for the poor, that is the idea that the Church's primary duty in a situation of oppression is to support the poor; (2) liberation is regarded as an essential element in salvation, since salvation is concerned with the whole man and not just his spiritual needs."[43] One source contributes the fact that "[Gutierrez] maintains that liberation entails a holistic process generated from spiritual experience; anything less is not genuine liberation."[44] Just as liberation theology seeks to make a holistic difference in the context of the oppressed, so this ministry to emerging adults seeks to make a holistic difference in the life of emerging adults thereby reinforcing the relevance of the church to their circumstance. However, "to its critics, liberation theology has reduced salvation to a purely worldly affair, and neglected its transcendent and eternal dimensions."[45] However, this is incorrect because merging adults need to see the connection of the faith they profess with the world in which they currently live along with the eternal ramifications of such profession. In its application to the model of ministry, this foundation provides necessary footing so as to address the relevance of the Christian faith to the whole person in part through praxis.

Scripture, in both the Old and New Testaments support this holistic emphasis within liberation theology. Beginning with the more recently written scripture in the New Testament, Thomas Hanks by "illustrating especially from James and Luke (Acts)…argues that liberation in the Bible is to be understood always holistically—freedom from sin, from illness, from demonic powers, from religious tyranny, from the poverty that springs from socio-economic and political oppression."[46] Again, this affiliation between liberation and wholeness supports the concept of the model of ministry addressing holistic concerns of emerging adult. In reference to the ministry of Jesus, David Baker correctly notes that Jesus preached "a gospel of liberation from suffering in this world (the horizontal or socio-economic aspect)" and also about "liberation from sin in this world and the world to come (the vertical or spiritual aspect)" thereby deducing that the "mission of the church today should include a holistic witness to the gospel, not concentrating exclusively on its social or its spiritual aspects."[47] This sort of balance in ministry is necessary in the church and therefore in the subset of ministry to emerging adults within the church context. According to Sutphin, liberation theologies share the perspective is:

> …that of salvation as total well-being in community with others. The Old Testament concept of 'shalom' (or wholeness) is often used to emphasize the social character of salvation and stress is placed upon salvation as a quality of the here and now. Sin, from this perspective, is interpreted as 'oppression,' as the opposite of liberation, as living without wholeness, or community.[48]

Sutphin also writes that the "goal of salvation for the Hebrew people was 'shalom,' a word which embraced a wide variety of meanings including peace, wholeness, prosperity, social, family, and personal well-being."[49] This along with the other scriptural references sustain the argument that holistic ministry is the appropriate type of ministry for the church and especially for a ministry to emerging adults seeking to find relevance in the church during this time of development. However, this last reference holds up the role of community in holistic salvation.

The emphasis of liberation theology on community is rightly noted in that "liberation theology is very dependent upon the support of the community of faith out of which it develops."[50] As a matter of fact, "Cone contends that theology is inseparable from the faith community. Theology presupposes that the reason for the community's being is given at the moment of its birth, and the task which theology has is to make clear to every succeeding generation the relevance of that original truth."[51] Here conveying the relevance of the truth is paramount and so it is in the model of ministry that seeks to leverage authentic community as a means to show the relevance of the gospel to the lives of emerging adults. This community exists not simply for the sake of being but for the purpose of dialogue defined as "mutual trust and respect" which "makes possible the development of true community."[52] Such an environment is necessary for developing authentic community and is critical for the attraction and the retention of emerging adults. Sutphin also writes "such participation and community is always possible, declares Russell, because Christ's presence with his people creates *koinonia* (fellowship, communion, sharing)."[53] Christ's presence makes these elements possible for the church at large, but also for emerging adult ministry in particular where these actions only strengthen the bonds between those in community further engraining in the psyche of involved emerging adults the relevance and importance of true Christian community. For it is absolutely true that "people need supportive communities in which to discover themselves if they are to attain full humanity."[54]

The liberation movement "itself was birthed from the lives of the downtrodden themselves in the context of the *comminidados ecclesiales de base* ('basic ecclesial communities'), Christian communes of the outcast who were attempting to relate their faith in a practical manner."[55] McCann writes that the "basic communities are characterized by a distinctive blend of religious and social concerns."[56] These communities consist of "small groups of people in particular localities who gather to pray, interpret the Bible together, and relate their faith to their common, everyday problems" and are "more communitarian than hierarchical in structure."[57] The importance of a community where faith and contextual issues converge for the purpose of dialogue cannot be overstated for the purposes of addressing emerging adult attraction and retention. By stressing commonality, emerging adults may forge greater bonds over what issues they share rather than focusing on the differences that could drive them apart. John McManners so eloquently summarizes this principle by noting the following, "When oppressed, dispirited people gather for religious comfort and in other-worldly hope, the sharing of their troubles and the articulating of their prayers creates a space within their lives where the warrant of their helplessness does not run, and they find a personal freedom and a corporate identity."[58] In other words, this authentic community not only benefits the individual, but also helps to shape a corporate identity. For the purposes of the model of ministry, such community could help redefine what has become normative religious individualist emerging adult behavior. Liberation theology demonstrates that emerging adults can come together in authentic community and help each other grow and cope with their common forms of oppression and hindrances to freedom.

With the role of community being so instrumental for liberation theology, it is important to note that different sources connect the principle of community with the church at large. For example, Russell Sutphin wrote that Letty Russell was "convinced that only when Christians understand salvation as a social and as an individual event, and begin to deal with the social issue that are obstacles to communication will the church really become the church."[59] This means that salvation from a holistic point of view helps the church address holistic concerns and fulfills the intent of Jesus who founded the church. The model of ministry designed to attract and retain emerging adults has to without fear confront the social issues about which emerging adults seek dialogue. Daniel Migliore also adds that the "model of the church as intimate community undoubtedly addresses real human needs."[60] If the church, and the model of ministry, addresses such needs it will lead to an authentic community where its members share their concerns with one another. To this point, Ronald Rolheiser writes that the "Christian scriptures speak of church community as somehow meaning a common life, of 'having everything in common.'"[61] He adds that common life in part means that Christians celebrate joys and fears while also being "responsible to each other and open to each other as regards mutual correction and challenge."[62] Mutual accountability is necessary for emerging adult attraction and retention, but this is only possible where there is authentic community.

Truly, ministry to emerging adults should include teaching, fellowship worship and outreach.[63] With regard to teaching, Setran and Kiesling are correct in noting that "to be truly transformative, such teaching must also be experiential, linking truth to life experience" to avoid making the mistakes experienced by interviewees in David Kinnaman's research who said that "church teaching was irrelevant to their careers and interests, failing to prepare them for 'real life.'"[64] Fellowship points to the importance of developing "strong biblical community" to emerging adult formation.[65] Truly, the "church must prompt and sustain deep worship, providing ample opportunities for emerging adults to abide in the presence of our supernatural God."[66] The church absolutely provides an "important setting for service, engaging emerging adults in work that looks beyond themselves to the needs of others within and outside the congregation."[67] These sources help articulate the connection between authentic community and the church and therefore also between ministry to emerging adults and community. In the context of community, Robert McAfee Brown asserts that it becomes necessary to create theologies, which are reactive to life situations without allowing these theologies to do nothing more than recapitulating such problems.[68] While according to Migliore, the "church no longer takes seriously the many forms of bondage from which human beings need to be liberated," the church must do so if it is to succeed in attracting and retaining emerging adults especially through the use of praxis.[69]

As discussed, although imperfect liberation theology suitably serves as a theological foundation for a model of ministry that addresses emerging adult attraction and retention due to its emphases on praxis, addressing holistic concerns, and doing so in the context of authentic community. Emerging adults need ministry that addresses their holistic concerns and that builds relationships to provide a platform for working through and shaping their theology during this formative time in their lives. Liberation theology still finds itself relevant for young adults and the church is an appropriate context for encounters that build the faith of emerging adults. Based on my observation, many emerging adults in the church seem oblivious to the interconnected natures of the spiritual and the secular, but a ministry partially founded upon the principles of liberation theology can connect the dots and lead to a greater holistic wellbeing. In the next chapter, I examine the opinions of scholars and authorities on the subject of emerging adult faith in the quest to inform a strategy for the attraction and retention of young adults.

NOTES

[1] Sinclair B. Ferguson and J.I. Packer, *New Dictionary of Theology* (Downers Grove, IL: InterVarsity Press, 2000), 388.

[2] F. L. Cross and Elizabeth A. Livingstone, *The Oxford Dictionary of the Christian Church* (New York, NY: Oxford University Press, 2005), 983.

³ David L. Smith, *A Handbook of Contemporary Theology: Tracing Trends & Discerning Directions in Today's Theological Landscape* (Grand Rapids, MI: BridgePoint Books, 1998), 209.

⁴ Ibid.

⁵ Gustavo Gutierrez, *A Theology of Liberation*, rev. ed. (Maryknoll, NY: Orbis Books, 1988), 103.

⁶ Carol Howard Merritt, *Tribal Church: Ministering to the Missing Generation* (Herndon, VA: The Alban Institute, 2007), 1.

⁷ J. Scott Horrell, Review of We Drink from Our Own Wells: The Spiritual Journey of a People, by Gustavo Gutierrez, *Themelios, No. 2, January 1986* 11 (1986): 70–71.

⁸ Leonardo Boff, *Faith on the Edge: Religion and Marginalized Existence*, trans. Robert R. Barr, (Maryknoll, NY: Orbis Books, 1991), 4.

⁹ Ibid., 59.

¹⁰ Ibid., 3-4.

¹¹ Ibid., 59.

¹² Ibid., 165.

¹³ Ibid.

¹⁴ Ibid., 106.

¹⁵ Ibid.

¹⁶ Ibid., 136.

¹⁷ Ibid., 202.

¹⁸ Ibid., 16.

¹⁹ Ibid., 26.

²⁰ Ibid., 195.

²¹ Smith, *A Handbook of Contemporary Theology*, 204.

²² Donald W. Musser and Joseph L. Price, *New and Enlarged Handbook of Christian Theology* (Nashville, TN: Abingdon Press, 2003), 300.

²³ Stanley T. Sutphin, *Options in Contemporary Theology* (Washington, D.C.: University Press of America, 1977), 44.

²⁴ Gareth Icenogle, *Biblical Foundations for Small Group Ministry* (Downers Grove, IL: InterVarsity Press, 1994), 118.

²⁵ Sutphin, 44.

²⁶ Ibid.

²⁷ Benner and Hill, *Baker Encyclopedia of Psychology & Counseling*, 686.

[28] Daniel G. Reid et al., *Dictionary of Christianity in America* s.v. "Liberation Theology," (Downers Grove, IL: InterVarsity Press, 1990).
[29] Ibid.
[30] Harvie M. Conn, "Theologies of Liberation: Towards a Common View," in *Tensions in Contemporary Theology*, 2nd ed., ed. Stanley N. Gundry and Alan F. Johnson (Grand Rapids, MI: Baker Book House, 1976), 400.
[31] LaVerne A. Rutschman, "Latin American Liberation Theology and Radical Anabaptism," *Journal Of Ecumenical Studies* 19, no. 1 (December 1, 1982): 44. *ATLA Religion Database with ATLASerials*, EBSCO*host* (accessed September 15, 2013).
[32] Dennis P. McCann, *Christian Realism and Liberation Theology: Practical Theologies in Creative Conflict* (Maryknoll, NY: Orbis Books, 1981), 148.
[33] June O'Connor, "Process Theology and Liberation Theology: Theological and Ethical Reflections." *Horizons* 7, no. 2 (September 1, 1980): 242. *ATLA Religion Database with ATLASerials*, EBSCO*host* (accessed September 15, 2013).
[34] Daniel G. Reid et al., *Dictionary of Christianity in America*, s.v. "Liberation Theology."
[35] Sutphin, 40.
[36] Ibid.
[37] Alister E. McGrath, *Christian Theology: An Introduction.* (West Sussex, UK: Wiley-Blackwell, 2011), 91.
[38] Leonardo Boff, *Jesus Christ Liberator: A Critical Christology for Our Time*. trans. Patrick Hughes. (Maryknoll, NY: Orbis Books, 1978), 275.
[39] Miroslav Volf, "Materiality of Salvation : An Investigation in the Soteriologies of Liberation and Pentecostal Theologies." *Journal Of Ecumenical Studies* 26, no. 3 (June 1, 1989): 447-467. *ATLA Religion Database with ATLASerials*, EBSCO*host* (accessed September 15, 2013), 455.
[40] David Tracy, *Plurality and Ambiguity: Hermeneutics, Religion and Hope* (San Francisco, CA: Harper & Row, 1987), 104.
[41] Sutphin, 44.
[42] Ibid.

[43] Cross and Livingstone, *The Oxford Dictionary of the Christian Church*, 983.
[44] Horrell, 70–71.
[45] McGrath, *Christian Theology*, 91.
[46] Francis Foulkes, "Review of God so Loved the Third World, by Thomas D. Hanks," *Themelios, No. 3, April 1984* 9 (1984): 35.
[47] David L. Baker, "The Jubilee and the Millennium," *Themelios, No. 1, October 1998* 24 (1998): 59.
[48] Sutphin, 40.
[49] Ibid., 58.
[50] Ibid., 39.
[51] Ibid., 47.
[52] Ibid., 41.
[53] Ibid., 60.
[54] Ibid., 57.
[55] Smith, *A Handbook of Contemporary Theology*, 208.
[56] McCann, *Christian Realism and Liberation Theology*, 142.
[57] Daniel L. Migliore, *Faith Seeking Understanding: An Introduction to Christian Theology*. 2nd. (Grand Rapids, MI: Wm. B. Eerdmans Publishing Co., 2004), 260.
[58] John McManners, ed., *The Oxford History of Christianity* (New York, NY: Oxford University Press, 1990), 660.
[59] Sutphin, 60.
[60] Migliore, 257.
[61] Ronald Rolheiser, *The Holy Longing: The Search for a Christian Spirituality* (New York, NY: Doubleday, 1999), 120.
[62] Ibid., 121.
[63] David P. Setran and Chris A. Kiesling, *Spiritual Formation in Emerging Adulthood: A Practical Theology for College and Young Adult Ministry* (Grand Rapids, MI: Baker Academic, 2013), 95.
[64] Ibid., 97.
[65] Ibid., 98.
[66] Ibid., 104.
[67] Ibid., 106.
[68] O'Connor, *Process Theology and Liberation Theology: Theological and Ethical Reflections*, 245.
[69] Migliore, 261.

CHAPTER FIVE
EXPERT VOICES ON EMERGING ADULTHOOD

    While addressing the issue of emerging adulthood attraction and retention necessitates biblical, historical and theological foundations, it also requires theoretical foundations or underpinnings found in disciplines outside of scripture, church history and systematic theology. To this end the pages that follow discuss varying publications and add their voices to the conversation of addressing this pressing issue for churches. Books as well as articles will be covered with regard to emerging adult spirituality and discuss models for keeping them involved in ministry through these personal times of transition.

    Many scholars including Jeffrey Arnett identified emerging adulthood to fall within the ages between eighteen and twenty-five. Arnett further indicates that the term "young adult" does not adequately describe persons that fall within the range of late teens to mid-twenties, therefore, they are referenced as emerging adults. While this is understandable, persons in their late-teens to mid-twenties face very adult situations even though they may not consider themselves to be adults. Emerging adulthood is a unique time in anyone's life. At this time, the "new family life cycle begins as the unattached young adult becomes an independent self and formulates personal life goals. During this stage the individual achieves some measure of emotional and financial independence from the family of origin.[1] Christian Smith writes that the "transition to adulthood today is more complex, disjointed, and confusing than in past decades" and that "these transitions are often accompanied by large doses of transience, confusion, anxiety, self-obsession, melodrama, conflict, disappointment, and sometimes emotional devastation."[2] In other words, "these young adults face problems others don't face."[3] Hayes lists as the three factors that persons need to keep in mind about young adults the facts that young adults believe little effort is necessary for instant gratification that "understanding information overload is key," and that young adults "are a generation of diversity."[4]

These years shape and mold the beliefs and values of young adults as well. Many young adults "have life goals that reflect more collectivistic values, emphasizing what they hope to do for others in the course of their lives."[5] This means they have the intent of having a positive and holistic impact on others that reflects a spirit of service. Another source writes that, "religious and political beliefs tend to be rather immature during the adolescent years" but "it is typically in the young adult years that these beliefs are internalized."[6] "Young adults are swimming in powerful cultural currents that work against maturation…There are implications here for discipleship and for Christians who teach, parent, pastor and work with emerging adults."[7] The pages that follow describe some of the research available regarding the faith development of emerging adults as well as prospective models for attracting and retaining emerging adults.

To Arnett, emerging adulthood is the "age of identity explorations, the age of instability, the self-focused age, the age of feeling in-between, and the age of possibilities."[8] During the years of emerging adulthood, young people develop a well-established worldview that has addressed concepts such as "God, death, right and wrong."[9] This means that this time is perhaps the most effective for helping to shape a person's worldview. Put another way, ministry in churches that helps in addressing these concepts can have a lasting impact upon these young persons for the rest of their lives. At the same time, the religious beliefs of emerging adults "have surprisingly little connection to their religious training in childhood and adolescence, a reflection of emerging adults' resolve to think for themselves and decide on their own beliefs."[10] Of those surveyed, Arnett found that 83% place some sort of importance on their religious beliefs, 74% say that religious faith bares some importance in their daily lives, 91% are at least somewhat certain of what they believe, and that 79% at least somewhat believe that God or a higher power watches over them and guides their lives.[11] But the same table also reports that 42% "indicated" that attend religious services was not important at all for them.[12] This means that while faith is important to emerging adults, many do not believe that attending religious service is necessary to evidence the importance of religion. This reflects the observations within churches and suggests that religious services alone will not be sufficient for attracting and retaining emerging adults.

Agreeably, "One reason the beliefs of many emerging adults are highly individualized is that they value thinking for themselves with regard to religious questions and believe it is important to form a unique set of religious beliefs rather than accepting a ready-made dogma."[13] This means that in order to attract and retain young adults, the church has to provide a safe space and empower them to think for themselves without telling them what they must believe or accept.

Oftentimes, in the context of focus teachers tell emerging adults what they should believe without encouraging them to think for themselves, as the model of ministry should have them. Arnett wrote that the "individualism valued by many emerging adults makes them skeptical of religious institutions and wary of being part of one."[14] This makes sense and so it follows that churches would do better to not require church membership in order for young adults to participate in church activities.

Apparently, young adults' "wariness of religious institutions is sometimes based on negative experiences that have led them to view such institutions as bastions of corruption and hypocrisy."[15] This is also a reason offered by young adults in churches, and so it is important for young adult attraction and retention that ministry leaders conduct themselves with integrity and humility. One phenomenon observed in churches is that young adults reject "religious participation in late adolescence or emergent adulthood" after attending religious services throughout childhood and early adolescence.[16] Based on the examples Arnett offered, forcing young persons to attend religious services normally backfires.[17] When young adults only attend services or participate in faith activities because they are following parental rules, this means that they must miss understanding faith's relevance to their lives. Helping young adults to see faith's relevance and the church's relevance to their lives can help in keeping them from rejecting religious participation when given the choice. Furthermore, the "main years of emerging adulthood, from age 18 to 25, are the nadir of religious participation in American society, and religious participation rises somewhat in the late twenties after many young people marry and have their first child."[18] Such research reflects the observed behavior of young adults to return to the church after marrying or having children. Arnett reported that in his research "on every measure of religiosity" African Americans "were more religious than other emerging adults" and that none interviewed were agonistic or atheist.[19] This means that for the primary African American congregation of interest that the situation for young adult retention and attraction is not as grave as it is for dissimilarly comprised congregations.

David Brooks refers to a portion of the period of emerging adulthood as the "odyssey" life phase that he defines as the "decade of wandering that frequently occurs between adolescence and adulthood."[20] Brooks called Robert Wuthnow's *After the Baby Boomers* "a tremendously valuable book…that looks at young adulthood through the prism of religious practice."[21] Wuthnow uses the term "younger adults" to describe persons between the ages of twenty-one and forty-five and rejects the notion that a singular pattern will be successful in attracting "young adults and grow" because this demographic is not a monolithic group.[22] "The single word that best describes young adults' approach to religion and spirituality—indeed life—is tinkering."[23] Wuthnow is absolutely right when he scribes that "religious traditions stay in business not only by making new recruits, but also by retaining their members."[24] "Retention is usually thought of by religious leaders as a matter of providing compelling teachings and sufficiently attractive programs to keep members from straying. However, human nature is often driven more by inertia than by persuasive reasons. If people are shielded from jarring incidents and from alluring opportunities, they typically stay the course."[25]

Rick Richardson has also tacked the issue of emerging adults with regard to their future participation in missional ministry. He refers to Robert Wuthnow's image of persons in their twenties tinkering with their faith and mentions that their embrace of "doctrines that make sense in a society that celebrates tolerance and scorns exclusion."[26] When attempting to attract and retain such persons who desire to create a custom belief system one must keep these facts in mind. Some of the hard lines on subjects such as soteriology and ecclesiology in many churches, according to Wuthnow, could be keeping emerging adults away. As observed emerging adults attempting to make sense of theology and make sense of the world in which they live have little patience for doctrines that do not make sense in society. Richardson also writes "in order for the Christian message to be received by emerging adults and by hosts and partners in mission as true, credible, or even moral, mission must be shaped so that it is attractive, good, and useful, contributing demonstrably to human flourishing... For emerging adults, mission must fully embrace integration of justice, compassion, relief, diversity, and witness."[27] Emerging adults, particularly in the subject context for this project recognize the holistic nature of the gospel, but many times only hear about the spiritual impacts of the Christian confession.

Christian Smith in *Souls in Transition* notes that the "ways emerging adult culture constructs the lives of most 18- to 29-year-olds simply seems to leave little room or felt need for God, faith, worship, prayer, community, or other forms of religious learning, practice, and service."[28] In fact, according to the evidence Smith presents "emerging adults are, on most sociological measures, the least religious adults in the United States today."[29] Judging by the lack of participation and faithfulness of the emerging adults in the context of model implementation, this is true. Even asking emerging adults if they see the relevance of the things Smith mentioned results in a negative response. However, Smith also found that religion for some emerging adults provides "stability, structure, support, and guidance."[30] The model of ministry needs to engage emerging adults and help them to share this sense of relevance. Writing about respondents who 'met God' or stumbled onto religious ideas and communities along the way, Smith notes that such persons are attracted to come back for more when they find "local communities of people who genuinely care about and for them."[31] This makes sense so much so that a model built with the intent of attracting and retaining young adults needs to lead its context in creating such a community.

Smith writing also in *Lost in Transition* accurately opines that "it is good for people to develop and enjoy loving relationships in community" and this is one of the "human goods" of which Smith calls emerging adults oblivious.[32] "Many religious congregations in fact devote significant resources to children and teenagers, yet unfortunately seem to passively accept that their ties to youth will be lost after the high school years" including the congregation of model implementation but in the words of Smith "this need not happen."[33] Smith is correct in that "there is no reason why churches...cannot more proactively sustain old ties and build new ones to local emerging adults, both those in college and those not in college."[34] In other words, a model intent on attracting and retaining emerging adult in a church is entirely feasible. Smith's model for accomplishing this goal includes "thoughtful panning, intentionality, investment, and sustained effort" all of which make sense. A ministry that does not possess each of these elements will likely fail at attracting and retaining emerging adults. Truly the congregation of interest, a religious community, can "do a much better job at connecting with emerging adults and supporting them" than it currently does and to do so would benefit the congregation "and the emerging adults involved."[35]

In interviews Christian Smith sheds additional light on emerging adults. In one of his responses he connects emerging adult faith with the activities directed toward teens and preteens suggesting that failing to resolve doubts during that time "will affect them later on."[36] He also notes that relationships between teenagers and "non-parental adults" such as the youth minister helps to strengthen "their faith over time."[37] In another interview, Smith is correct "in terms of the implications of our work for churches, the two keywords are engagement and relationships. It can't just be programs or classes or handing them over to the youth pastor. Real change happens in relationships, and that takes active engagement."[38] Building relationships in churches among emerging adults are critical for emerging adult faith. Smith is also correct in asserting that "to connect with emerging adults is going to take more creativity and initiative" than he initially saw, and that success in ministry will require more "ways to form communities and places where people can connect and work out common interests beyond the standard worship service and Sunday school."[39] In reference to Hintz's point about single young adults who desire and seek companionship, he also wrote that the "church must provide it, or they will go where it is available, even that of the wrong kind. The minister must find ways to reach them, though this is not always easy. It may be necessary to arrange for appointments beforehand."[40]

Carol Howard Merritt's book *Tribal Church: Ministering to the Missing Generation* sets out for a model for an entire church that will bless young adults rather than a blueprint for a young adult ministry. The writer is identifiable because she also is a young adult seeking to lead other young adults into greater faith. This resource is valuable for the ministry model because it led to a reversal of the "trend of lost membership" and led to keeping the original members and a "consistent ten percent growth made up of individuals of various ages."[41] Merritt rightly posits "others in their twenties and thirties are still searching for a space where they can nurture their connection with God and community without having to hide their progressive viewpoints."[42] Emerging adults in churches seem to hold more progressive viewpoints, but may resist sharing for the fear of condemnation. The model of ministry should, therefore, be required to provide a safe space for sharing potentially controversial topics. Emerging adults need community because "adults in their twenties and thirties often do not have friends or family surrounding them in networks of support," but what Merritt calls the tribal church "realizes this and pays attention to the young adult's general well-being."[43] This attention to the holistic concern regarding emerging adults is largely missing from churches. According to Merritt, it is "no longer important for someone in their twenties or thirties to go to church."[44] Young adults shun religion because practicing religion "has become synonymous with being small-minded, belligerent, arrogant, perverse, and even violent" causing "younger generations to distance themselves from religion."[45] By establishing and supporting a nurturing community, the model of ministry could lead the church to redefining religion for emerging adults. Sadly, the "church lets go of young people when they need spiritual grounding the most," times such as starting a career or leaving home for college because the church focuses on caring for the babies and the elderly, but "give up on anything in between."[46] As observed, Baptist churches, and in particular the church of implementation, are not the only denominations that wrestle with young adults taking a "twenty-year hibernation period from the church."[47]

Tribal church is "a term for a subculture, a network of relationships, or a group of people who care for each other in the most basic ways" that "understands and reaches out to the nomadic culture of young adults. This church responds to the gifts and needs of adults under forty by taking into account their physical, social, and spiritual circumstance."[48] This holistic approach of responding to the holistic needs of adults is most beneficial and key for adults seeing the relevance of ministry for their lives. In order to have a thriving population of young adults, Merritt suggests that the environment must include rather than seeking to exclude persons for reasons such as sexual lifestyles and religion.[49] Young adults "see their duty as spiritual people as being to treat others as they would like to be treated, and that means that they don't tolerate intolerance."[50] Many seem to be more concerned with the spirit behind religion than religious structure. For example, young adults are "less concerned with obtaining a true literal interpretation of the Bible," but instead are more concerned with practical application of the text and practical theology.[51] Persons leading emerging adults, therefore, should be trained to deal with both an appropriate interpretation and the practical application of the text. Merritt also offers as a strategy the concept of promoting shared leadership or providing leadership opportunities for young adults as a means to keep young adults involved in the church. Additionally, she suggests that letting a young person run the church will keep her or him engaged just as leadership keeps others in their sixties involved.[52] Sadly, in many churches the voices of young adults in the church at large are muted. Merritt truthfully writes that to reach young adults, preachers must build a "hermeneutical bridge" which leads to sermons that speak to the issues and concerns of young adults.[53] This source is very helpful in detailing practices that have been successful in attracting and retaining young adults by building community and helping them understand the relevance of the church to their young adult lives.

Ralph Watkins' book *The Gospel Remix: Reaching the Hip Hop Generation* discusses the particular challenge of reaching the hip-hop generation. A portion of the eighteen to thirty demographic is covered by what Ralph Watkins calls the hip-hop generation or young adults using Bakari Kitwana's definition of the hip-hop generation as persons born between 1965 and 1986.[54] The model of ministry should need to be a welcoming place that seeks to include rather than exclude based on arbitrary rules such as minimum membership standards for participation.[55] The author is right in that "for a church to be effective in evangelism, the church must be willing to change. But the change that a church makes must be rooted in the Word of God" meaning rooted in Jesus and the Bible.[56] Watkins asks a lot of questions for the purpose of evaluation and to get leaders thinking about how their own context might embrace the hip-hop generation. He suggested that making changes to minister to this generation would run into some resistance in the form of what he calls dissenters or those who do not agree with the church's efforts to "reach the hip-hop generation."[57] Watkins is on target when he writes that the "hip-hop generation is looking for spiritual encounters that get them in touch with their feelings, encounters with the holy that are relevant, encounters that are applicable to their circumstances and aren't shrouded in religious language."[58] He is also correct in noting that the "hip-hop generation also wants the freedom to talk back to religious leaders and to God…looking for dialogue—not monologues."[59] More emphasis needs to rest in teaching for the model of ministry because "teaching churches have done well with young adults because the best of teaching churches encourage their people to think."[60]

Watkins adds another voice to the debate concerning emerging adults in his collaboration with Benjamin Stephens in *From Jay-Z to Jesus: Reaching and Teaching Young Adults in the Black Church*. To this point, they were correct in writing that "churches that are intentional in developing young adult ministry will see an influx of young adults seeking an informed faith that speaks to both head and heart. Young adults want to be able to ask questions without rebuke but with a loving, informed answer that engages sacred text while respecting their personal journeys."[61] This agrees with the model design of having a supportive community that addresses concerns relevant to emerging adults. Adding to the complexity of addressing this issue is the conundrum that many young adults face as articulated by Stephens and Watkins:

> In the midst of divergent religious worldviews, young adults who consider themselves Christians are trying not to be judgmental and closed-minded while simultaneously trying to believe there is only one name by which people might he saved. They are sitting at the crossroads of faith not knowing how to engage in civil conversation about such important topics. They wonder how to negotiate this diverse religious

terrain while both following and being critical of their parents' faith.[62]

Stephens and Watkins followed my train of thinking in asserting that "preaching must be relevant" and that "young adults want to hear sermons that are relevant to the wider cultural situation."[63] In addition, young adults "want to be actively engaged in what they see as meaningful ministry, and they want to see their dollars make a tangible difference in the lives of others."[64]

Jimmy Long begins his book *Emerging Hope* about reaching postmodern generations in a way similar to other authors by discussing many of the challenges or characteristics that describe emerging adults. The emerging adults in his context are Millennials as distinguished from Gen Xers, but both groups yearn for community as evidenced by their extended families comprised of friends.[65] Long is correct in asserting, "to minister effectively among these younger generations, we must understand and truly appreciate the distinctives of these generations and the diversity of people within them."[66] Furthermore, he accurately posits, "a vibrant Christian community can provide a critical dimension in reaching the emerging postmodern world with the gospel and in caring for new Christians after they have made a commitment to the gospel."[67] Many churches have room for improvement in this area. Long further notes that "Christians need to enter into true Christian community, caring for each other and reaching out to others outside the community."[68] This seems to suggest that community is critical in being able to reach out to others perhaps for the purpose of attracting them to the Christian community itself. The sense of individualism among emerging adults in churches hinders such community and therefore hinders the growth of the emerging adult population of the congregation in question. Truthfully, since "'homily' is derived from the Greek word for 'conversation,'" if preaching is to reach emerging adults it should "nurture the community's conversation about meaning in light of their life together and shared tradition."[69] It makes sense that "because of their commitment to community, [people in the emerging culture] are impressed with the truth lived out in community. This demonstration of the truth in community is convincing to a postmodern mindset. Therefore, evangelism is only possible when the community doing the evangelism lives out the Christian message. The medium is the message."[70]

In their book *Getting Real: An Interactive Guide to Relational Ministry* authors Ken Baugh and Rich Hurst are correct in noting that young adults "value real conversation about real issues and real responsibilities" and that "many young adults want to create their own ministries, something that reflects them."[71] This is possible through the use of context associates in the model of ministry who are emerging adults themselves. According to Baugh and Hurst, the two key elements of programming are transformational communities and building programs that work. The authors emphasize the role of community in young adult ministry while defining community as a "place where people know your fears, failures, and dreams but love you anyway."[72] Baugh and Hurst write that transformational communities are the answer to the question of how ministries may "create safe relationships where this generation can heal and come to know and experience the love of God."[73] Such communities are places where young adults are enabled to be real without fear of judgment or rejection.[74] Truly, transformational communities are necessary for reaching and ministering to emerging adults. This theory undergirds the notion that a model of ministry seeking to attract and retain emerging adults must create such transformational community. Building transformational community is one particular possibility for growth in churches. Authors Baugh and Hurst also discuss "four basic programming purposes" for a "people-driven model of ministry."[75]

These include the quadrants of attracting, involving ("connecting people into the ministry"), reproducing ("equipping, discipling, mentoring, and leadership development,") and multiplying (using outreach to grow the ministry).[76] This means that specific programs will be necessary in the model of ministry focused on attraction and retention in order to accomplish the individual goals of these quadrants.

In their book *Spiritual Formation in Emerging Adulthood*, David Setran and Chris Kiesling notes "at this time of life, emerging adults move beyond authority-bound structures and begin owning and internalizing faith commitments. Yet this process, [they] contend is fostered not by complete autonomy and separation from authority structures but within 'communities of truth' that bestow Christian identity on emerging adults."[77] Therefore, Setran and Kiesling come to the agreeable position that "ministries and churches have a responsibility to help emerging adults own adult identities within communities of faith ... marked by prayer, dedication, and communal promises of support, such experiences can serve as powerful markers to motivate and provide meaning for the adult Christian life."[78] Some blame emerging adult disengagement from the church on emerging adults themselves or on local churches but "while few agree on the sources of decline, the result is clear: a loss of corporate spiritual formation and guidance at the very time when key life decisions are made."[79] In response, Setran and Kiesling "offer practical suggestions for emerging adults and for churches seeking to enhance their focus on this formative period of life."[80] For example, "communal formation through the local congregation can serve as one of the most powerful forces of spiritual growth in emerging adults' lives, countering many of the deforming beliefs, attitudes, and behaviors endemic to this stage, while forming them in ways that lead to mature adult faith."[81] Setran and Kiesling are correct in writing that the "threads of spiritual formation, identity, church participation, vocation, morality, relational wholeness, and mentoring can create a tapestry, however imperfect, of costly discipleship, community, and mission."[82]

According to Richard Flory and Donald Miller's in *GenX Religion*, "GenXers" would have included some of those that fall into this work's definition of emerging adults who at the time of this book's publishing fell into the range of nineteen to thirty-nine years of age.[83] They write that "although boomers and GenXers are religious seekers, Xer seeking is more than just a quest for an individualistic spiritual experience-Xers are instead looking for and creating community, belonging, and authenticity, which can only be measured within the religious community."[84] The authors emphasize greatly the importance of building community for this generation and churches needs such a community to support the spiritual development of emerging adults in the hopes that they will remain and attract others during their years of emerging adulthood and beyond.

Most of the young adults in the predefined criteria belong to the Millennial generation as defined by Mike Hayes in *Googling God* as persons born after 1980 and the majority of these persons would fall into the category of emerging adulthood.[85] He also writes that young adults "seek a theology that is more contemplative and even more demanding of them."[86] Rather than perceived as dumbing down Christianity, this means that model of ministry needs to encourage deep thought and not dispense with structure or standards with the expectation that doing so is necessary for attracting and or retaining emerging adults. Millennials "find comfort in homogeneous community."[87] Hayes identifies seven identifications or classifications of young adults to include eclipsed, private, ecumenical, evangelical, sacramental, prophetic and communal.[88]

For each of these the author describes methods that have been effective in reaching young adults in chapter two. Seemingly it would take a ministry that took these categories into consideration in order to appeal to the young adult population and to minister to the emerging adults already present in churches. Approaches that work well include intentionally aiming ministry "at those young adults who return to the church after an absence," "a need for a digital spirit in ministry," "a ministry that is open to dialogue," "a ministry that is rooted in my" and tradition, a ministry concerned with social justice, and "a ministry that provides life-giving community."[89] This describes a young adult ministry with a holistic view of the world that provides a community of young adults with whom other young adults "wish to associate."[90] Hayes also writes that for Millennials as well as Generation X, there is a "need for a nonjudgmental community."[91]

Hayes is correct in asserting that it is the job of the minister to young adults to "find out where they are going. This will provide [ministers] with many ideas on how to connect with them later on."[92] At the same time, effective ministry—in this case ministry to emerging adults already present in the church—is its own best advertisement as Hayes notes, "when young adults experience solid ministry, the news spreads like wildfire. Suddenly new people are checking in, wondering what the buzz is about."[93] Hayes also rightly highlights the fact that ministers to young adults "need to continually invite young adults into [their] ministry opportunities. This is an indispensable part of ministry. Not only do the clergy and the lay ministry staff need to do the inviting, but they need to encourage and even demand that young adults involved in ministry continue to invite people to join them."[94] In order to attract emerging adults leaders and ministry participants need to invite them to come because if they do not demonstrate or communicate the benefits or excitement surrounding such ministry, emerging adults will be less likely to attend. Hayes rightly also communicates that ministries to young adults should in fact provide safe spaces, communal places of confidentiality and support, for young adults.[95]

The young adults profiled in Colleen Carroll's book *The New Faithful*, were born between the years of 1965 and 1983 with the young ones falling into what she calls Generation Y.[96] Some of these persons would fall into this work's definition of emerging adults. "Young adults need support to make faith commitments that last."[97] "Young adults themselves, not to mention the throngs of sociologists seeking to understand them, repeatedly refer to their quest for authentic, intimate communities."[98] "Young believers often join faith communities that help them stay committed. Eventually, many of them became witnesses to those very same gospel values that led them to conversion and that can, in turn, lead their peers to conversion. That cycle of personal and communal witness has the potential to transform American Christianity and the face of a generation searching for substance."[99] "Authentic Christian communities…do not make it easy on young adults."[100] Carroll describes these communities as "sacrificial, demanding radical commitment, selflessness, and personal growth" while also being "incarnational," "intimate," and "evangelical."[101] She is correct and such communities are necessary for the ministry focus.

Typical other books on the subject, Sharon Park's book *Big Questions, Worthy Dreams* discusses the difficulty of defining young adulthood before speaking of the unique characteristics of a group she seems to place in the range of seventeen to thirty.[102] Park's assertions that "networks of belonging provide the trustworthy holding upon which all humans depend for their flourishing within the wider world and the universe it spins through," and that "faith is a patterning, connective, relational activity embodied and shaped not within the individual alone, but in the comfort and challenges of the company we keep" are on target and helpful for the context in question.[103] "The communion features of the psyche at the threshold of adulthood remain in focus" when remembering that young adults have "two great yearnings" including the yearning to exercise "one's own power to make a difference" and the "yearning for belonging, connection, inclusion, relationship, and intimacy."[104] According to Park, "for the young adult, community finds its most powerful form in a mentoring community."[105] To this end she also writes, "it is vital to recognize that a network of belonging that serves young adults as a mentoring environment may offer a powerful milieu and a critical set of gifts in the formation of meaning, purpose, and faith."[106] In leading churches to greater wholeness with regard to emerging adults Park's point must be kept in mind. Park rightly prescribes that young adults need faith communities that "Extend hospitality to big questions; recognize the claims of a plurality of religious traditions; create a meaningful network of belonging, comfort, and ethical challenge; give access to viable stories and myths, symbols, and songs; recognize the promise and contributions of young adult lives; evoke worthy Dreams; and hold mentors and young adults alike in a viable hope."[107]

The published work entitled *Virtual Faith* by Thomas Beaudoin covers the faith development of Generation X or those in their twenties and thirties at the time of the book's composition.[108] Part of this demographic would fit the parameters for emerging adulthood. Beaudoin discusses the issues that affect young adults throughout his book. Truthfully in this technological age, "technology enables intimate discussion about spirituality, which benefits both Xers and Net-based ministries."[109] Therefore, the model of ministry should leverage technology for the purpose of intimate communication and dissemination of information. For the benefit of the church that implements a ministry for emerging adults, it may be helpful to form a version of Beaudoin's "Saving Remnant" where a "group of faithful people who will renew the larger community."[110] Virtual communities, especially when combined with face-to-face interactions can facilitate more frank and "self-revelatory" discussions.[111] This should be combined with face-to-face interactions in the model of ministry so as to form virtual and in-person intimate communities.

In his article "Narrative discipleship," Nathan Byrd utilizes Arnett's definition of emerging adulthood to include the "period of life between 18 and 30."[112] He articulates the problem well by noting that "teenagers and 20-something young adults are leaving the churches of their childhood in record numbers" and that "despite some very ambitious attempts, most traditional churches are not successful in keeping young adults in congregations or converting the non-religious to become people of faith."[113] This research reflects the reality of the context in question. Byrd's argument that narrative discipleship has merit where he notes that eliciting and then interpreting personal stories can be effective in discipling young adults.[114] Byrd also accurately writes that "walking with a young or emerging adult through the process of narrating his or her faith journey takes time as well as skillful questioning and listening."[115] Using "narrative discipleship may assist ministers, educators, and volunteers in making faith more relevant for contemporary emerging adults after college graduation."[116]

In *Essential Church*, the authors note the lack of relevance of church for many by writing that according to such persons "church is not essential to their lives."[117] The authors' "journey started with a study of eighteen- to thirty-year-old adults in America" and they found that "more than two-thirds of young churchgoing adults in America drop out of church between the ages of eighteen and twenty-two!"[118] This research is not a surprise based on previously observed behavior. Rainer and Rainer are absolutely correct as they acknowledge that "young adults are likely to stay in the church if they see church as essential to their lives" and describe churches that have been effective in retaining young adults by communicating how essential the church is to young adult lives.[119] The strategies for implementing essential churches involves "simplify," "deepen," "expect," and "multiply" or to get the structure, content, attitude and action right respectively.[120]

The book also highlights an issue in the context that the "church, which is supposed to be the locus of community, does not provide a sense of community for many of the dechurched. And as a consequence, these young people move to different places to connect with others. They are looking for a different kind of community. This generation desires an essential connection with others."[121] The authors correctly notes that "when churches begin to focus on how to reach the community instead of spending all their time on existing programs and people, the current people of the church grow stronger."[122] Making them work together in attracting others strengthens the bond between them.

Sundene and Dunn write that "for our purposes, however, we will use the terms 'young adult' and 'emerging adult' interchangeably to refer to adults ranging from ages nineteen to thirty-five."[123] The authors write that:

> While emerging adults all over the globe share the same developmental journey as [Richard's daughter Jessica], her connection to a vibrant relational spiritual community is atypical for young adults we've observed in cultures all over the world. Rarely does a week go by without both of us encountering a young adult longing for and lacking a relation-ship that will encourage and facilitate spiritual maturity in Christ.[124]

This reinforces the importance of community for spiritual formation of emerging adults. The authors prescribe a strategy that has potential for "shaping the church and changing the world" and that is "shaping the "next generation through disciplemaking" because they are "convinced, therefore, that this relational strategy is mission-critical to the future of the church in the world."[125] The authors also rightly suggest that, "authentic Christian community also provides a crucial link in learning about purpose and contribution."[126] Furthermore, "experimental risk-taking is not only possible but even desirable; the emerging adult wants to be challenged, supported and empowered. The church that attempts to cater to them, then, by trying harder and harder to attract them, will ultimately drive them away."[127] The model of ministry then must facilitate a community that meets such desires if it is to attract emerging adults instead of continuing to succeed in pushing them away.

Bowers' *Designing Contemporary Congregations* overall suggests that changing is the key to the church's survival and relevance. The postmodern generation, according to Bowers, includes those whose parents grew up in the 1960s that should place such persons in the realm of Arnett's definition of emerging adults.[128] Young adults are "suspicious of the church's evangelism," and they typically prefer the term "spirituality" to distinguish their religion from the "religion that is preached by an authority figure within a religious organization."[129] To the postmodern, religion is an "internal process that can be practiced anywhere" as opposed to perceiving religion, in the way of the modern worshiper, as a "collective practice within the walls of organized religion."[130] She also writes, "no postmodern believer is going to be drawn to a depressed organization."[131] Bowers defines this depression as a "lack of spiritual energy" or the "creative energy to transform itself, to heal organizational struggles, and to promote itself as a major player in the cultural environment."[132] The "most effective way to attract the postmodern generation is to focus on healing congregational depression."[133] Bowers is correct that "attracting and assimilating the postmodern believer in to the life of the congregation and empowering the postmodern believer to determine the design of the contemporary congregation will also help alleviate the congregation's depression."[134] "The postmodern generation will only be attracted to the contemporary congregation if it is receptive to change to access energy and to grow spiritually."[135] Churches must implement such changes and provide such support if it is to rise from its congregational depression and begin to attract emerging adults.

Donna Thoennes writes on the topic of community and its importance to college aged students—a portion of the emerging adult population—in her article "Keeping it Real." She writes that a symptom of the crisis in higher education highlighted in research by Willimon and Naylor is "the absence of community. Students continue to communicate a longing for connectedness and relationships. They are no longer seeking freedom but belonging."[136] Among the seven themes, which surfaced in the research in the form of student interviews, of particular interest are the themes of leadership, interaction, activities, and authenticity.[137] With regard to authenticity, Thoennes writes that:

> One of the identifying markers of a true community is an individual's awareness that she is known by others. Such knowledge is highly valued because it results in the individual feeling loved. One's knowledge of another is contingent upon whether that person is willing to share her weaknesses and needs. The kind of sharing students desire involves mutual trust and sensitivity to hear the needs and struggles of others.[138]

Such a sense of awareness is critical for the success of the model of ministry. Coupled with this sense of awareness is the necessity for a community free of judgment where persons "accept rather than judge" others in community critically.[139]

In addition to the works mentioned previously, the works as the result of the Changing Spirituality of Emerging Adults Project offer valuable contributions to this discussion. For example, Conrad Hackett noted that "less than a third of congregations" meet the threshold of having 10% emerging adults, and that "considering the characteristics of these congregations will provide clues about which factors could help attract and retain emerging adults."[140] He also stated that, "While emerging adults value many of the same traits in their congregation as older adults, they place greater emphasis on nontraditional worship styles, evangelism, social activities, and diversity. Emerging adults tend to be concentrated in congregations that are larger and have more men, greater racial diversity, and members with more conservative theology."[141] The model of ministry was designed with these traits in mind specifically those of social activities and diversity at least with regard to ages in the range of emerging adult hood. Penny Edgell also contributed to the discussion by adding "today's emerging adults are less involved in organized religion than are older adults."[142] Further characterizing emerging adults, she noted that:

> It was once common for sociologists to argue that even if young adults 'dropped out' of religion in their late teens or early 20s, they would 'come back' once they were married and started having children. But it is not clear that 'coming back' is the right way to think about the religious trajectories of emerging adults…And for all emerging adults, it is unclear whether coming back to participation in organized religion is the automatic choice once one has lived for up to a decade without religious involvement."[143]

Also, Annette Mahoney raises legitimate concerns when in reference to headlines that highlight religious persons involved in scandals she wrote:

> With headlines like these, many emerging adults may doubt whether religion offers anything to strengthen American marriages and families. Hypocrisy seems to abound. Leaders of evangelical Christians (about 25% of the U.S. population) seem to dominate the airwaves on faith and family. "Christianity" often seems synonymous with Biblical fundamentalist rhetoric that elevates one particular type of family to a social and sacred pedestal—namely, the 1950s middle-class vision of a breadwinner father married to a stay-at-home mother of their biological offspring. Could this be one reason emerging adults flee organized religion?[144]

In addition, in their article "Friends and Friendships in Emerging Adulthood" Carolyn McNamara Barry and Stephanie D. Madsen write about the importance of friendship to the development of emerging adults. They write that "friends can be a proxy family for young people, offering invaluable advice, support, and companionship," "friendships are central to the lives of emerging adults," and "friends help people to figure themselves out and influence their behavior, potentially for both good and bad."[145] Further they stated that, "friends support emerging adults' identity development. Friendships provide feelings of worth as well as opportunities for story telling and frank discussions about religion, life aspirations, moral dilemmas, and relationships."[146] This essay accurately notes that "friendships involve intimacy and interdependence" and "friends' behaviors affect emerging adults' positive outcomes, including church attendance."[147] By seeking to establish firm communal relationships, the model of ministry should align the thought of Barry and Madsen.

Gary McIntosh defined Busters as those persons "born between 1965 and 1983" and at the time of publishing persons in this group ranged from nineteen to thirty-seven years of age.[148] This range covers the majority of the population targeted by this model (eighteen to thirty). McIntosh had a point when he wrote "church leaders must overcome past prejudices and begin to reach out to Busters with the acceptance and love commanded by Christ"[149] because they "long to be accepted for who they are and to know that they matter to God."[150] "The church of the 2020s and beyond will be led by Busters, so it is vitally important that we understand and minister to them today."[151] Busters "value a true family atmosphere" due to a number of factors, and family to them includes "practically anyone who will be their friend."[152] While each of McIntosh's concepts for reaching unchurched Busters is insightful, number two which dealt with "relationally, nothing captivates Busters more than friends and family" stood out the most.[153] McIntosh correctly noted that a sense of belonging undergirded by "family-style activities" and group discussions bears importance for Busters.[154]

"Busters want their own needs met" and "they want a faith that works for them."[155] McIntosh also noted that the "lack of strong support networks or moral ethics has resulted in a problem-ridden generation" which leads Busters to "look for a church that will nurture them and give them practical resources to survive in a post-Christian culture."[156] In addition, "Busters want to meet the real needs of other people. They expect churches to be concerned about and involved with the social, political, and environmental issues of their local communities."[157] This seems to mean that members of that generation have a holistic perspective with regard to the work in which they believe the church should participate. "The best way to touch their hearts for Christ is to simply spend time doing things with them. Taking time to play basketball or a table game will do more to open their hearts to the gospel than will most church services."[158] "Churches that have honest, straightforward, tell-it-like-it-is worship services seem to attract Busters. Worship services can be short or long, just so they are real and not considered a waste of time."[159] Interestingly, "a study that was reported in June 2001 found that young adults aged eighteen to twenty-nine are the least likely to attend church."[160]

Each of the aforementioned sources as well as others not cited contribute valuable information to the conversation of leading the church in question into wholeness by addressing the issue of emerging adult attraction and retention. While it is impossible to agree with every author's perspective or to integrate every sound suggestion into a model of ministry, the model will take the principles articulated by these authors into consideration upon model design. One may expect that others will continue to investigate this issue and so this foundation will need to be adapted as others shed more light on the religiosity of emerging adults as well as what is effective in attracting and retaining young adults.

These sources present a comprehensive view not only of the spiritual development of emerging adults, but what it may take to increase their level of religious commitment to include the establishment of authentic community. Truly, "young adults, like other members of the population, need to find and experience authentic connection in their everyday lives."[161] Kiesling accurately captures one of the themes of the research by noting that the "journey toward wholeness involves finding a spiritual community that fosters plausibility for the Christian life."[162] While emerging adults are not a monolithic group, these sources foster hope in the premise that the church can succeed in attracting and retaining emerging adults after coming to understand the nuances of this particular demographic. Now that the book has explored various foundations, the subsequent chapter covers the model of ministry designed after conversing with these sources and reveals a recipe for emerging adult attraction and retention.

NOTES

[1] David G. Benner and Peter C. Hill, eds., *Baker Encyclopedia of Psychology & Counseling*, Baker Reference Library (Grand Rapids, MI: Baker Books, 1999), 437.

[2] Christian Smith, *Souls in Transition: The Religious and Spiritual Lives of Emerging Adults* (New York, NY: Oxford University Press, 2009), 6.

[3] August W. Hintz, "The Pastor as Friend," ed. Ralph G. Turnbull, *Baker's Dictionary of Practical Theology* (Grand Rapids, MI: Baker Book House, 1967), 327.

⁴ Mike Hayes, introduction in *Googling God: The Religious Landscape of People in their 20s and 30s* (Mahwah, NJ: Paulist Press, 2007), xii.
⁵ Jeffrey Jensen Arnett, *Adolescence and Emerging Adulthood: A Cultural Approach*, 3rd (Upper Saddle River, NJ: Pearson, 2007), 183.
⁶ Benner and Hill, *Baker Encyclopedia of Psychology & Counseling*, 47.
⁷ Beth Felker Jones, "Emerging as Adults," *Christian Century* 129, no. 25 (December 12, 2012): 44. *ATLA Religion Database with ATLASerials*, EBSCOhost (accessed September 28, 2013).
⁸ Arnett, 45.
⁹ Ibid., 166.
¹⁰ Ibid., 166-167.
¹¹ Ibid., 168.
¹² Ibid.
¹³ Ibid., 172.
¹⁴ Ibid.
¹⁵ Ibid., 173.
¹⁶ Ibid., 176.
¹⁷ Ibid.
¹⁸ Ibid., 177.
¹⁹ Ibid., 178.
²⁰ David Brooks, "The Odyssey Years," *New York Times*, October 9, 2007, accessed October 28, 2013, http://www.nytimes.com/2007/10/09/opinion/09brooks.html?_r=0.
²¹ Ibid.
²² Robert Wuthnow, *After the Baby Boomers: How Twenty and Thirty-Somethings Are Shaping the Future of American Religion* (Princeton, NJ: Princeton University Press, 2007), 5-6.
²³ Ibid., 13.
²⁴ Ibid., 81.
²⁵ Ibid.
²⁶ Rick Richardson, "Emerging Adults and the Future of Missions," *International Bulletin Of Missionary Research* 37, no. 2 (April 1, 2013): 79. *ATLA Religion Database with ATLASerials*, EBSCOhost (accessed September 25, 2013).
²⁷ Ibid., 84.

[28] Smith, *Souls in Transition*, 82.
[29] Ibid., 102.
[30] Ibid., 84-85.
[31] Ibid., 85.
[32] Christian Smith, *Lost in Transition: The Dark Side of Emerging Adulthood* (New York, NY: Oxford University Press, 2011), 9.
[33] Smith, *Lost in Transition*, 241.
[34] Ibid.
[35] Ibid., 241-242.
[36] Christian Smith and Jane Thayer, "Inside Story of a Landmark Study on the Religious and Spiritual Lives of Emerging Adults: An Interview with Christian Smith." *Christian Education Journal* 8, no. 2 (September 1, 2011): 336. *ATLA Religion Database with ATLASerials, EBSCOhost* (accessed September 28, 2013).
[37] Ibid.
[38] Katelyn Beaty and Christian Smith, "Lost in Transition: with his Latest Research on Emerging Adults, Sociologist Christian Smith Helps the Church Reach out to a Rootless Generation," *Christianity Today* 53, no. 10 (October 1, 2009): 37. *ATLA Religion Database with ATLASerials, EBSCOhost* (accessed September 28, 2013).
[39] Ibid.
[40] Hintz, 327.
[41] Carol Howard Merritt, *Tribal Church: Ministering to the Missing Generation* (Herndon, VA: The Alban Institute, 2007), 15.
[42] Ibid., 3.
[43] Ibid., 8.
[44] Ibid., 16.
[45] Ibid., 73.
[46] Ibid., 90.
[47] Ibid.
[48] Ibid., 7-8.
[49] Ibid., 62-63.
[50] Ibid., 63.
[51] Ibid., 73.
[52] Ibid., 94.
[53] Ibid., 127.
[54] Ralph C. Watkins, *The Gospel Remix: Reaching the Hip Hop Generation* (Valley Forge, PA: Judson Press, 2007), 12.

⁵⁵ Ibid., 23.
⁵⁶ Ibid., 46.
⁵⁷ Ibid., 59.
⁵⁸ Ibid., 62.
⁵⁹ Ibid.
⁶⁰ Ibid., 65.
⁶¹ Benjamin Stephens III and Ralph C. Watkins, *From Jay-Z to Jesus: Reaching and Teaching Young Adults in the Black Church* (Valley Forge, PA: Judson Press, 2009), 8.
⁶² Ibid., 15.
⁶³ Ibid., 83.
⁶⁴ Ibid., 88.
⁶⁵ Jimmy Long, *Emerging Hope: A Strategy for Reaching Postmodern Generations*, 2nd ed., (Downers Grove, IL: InterVarsity Press, 2004), 51-52.
⁶⁶ Ibid., 54.
⁶⁷ Ibid., 77.
⁶⁸ Ibid., 85.
⁶⁹ David Lose, *Confessing Jesus Christ: Preaching in a Postmodern World* (Grand Rapids, MI: Eerdmans, 2003), 129.
⁷⁰ Long, 206.
⁷¹ Ken Baugh and Rich Hurst, *Getting Real: An Interactive Guide to Relational Ministry* (Colorado Springs, CO: NavPress, 2000), xvii.
⁷² Ibid., 15.
⁷³ Ibid., 117.
⁷⁴ Ibid., 118.
⁷⁵ Ibid., 133.
⁷⁶ Ibid., 133-134.
⁷⁷ David P. Setran and Chris A. Kiesling, *Spiritual Formation in Emerging Adulthood: A Practical Theology for College and Young Adult Ministry* (Grand Rapids, MI: Baker Academic, 2013), 8.
⁷⁸ Ibid., 77.
⁷⁹ Ibid., 82.
⁸⁰ Ibid., 8.
⁸¹ Ibid., 95.
⁸² Ibid., 239.

[83] Richard W. Flory and Donald E. Miller, eds., *GenX Religion* (New York, NY: Routledge, 2000), 3.
[84] Ibid., 244.
[85] Hayes, xi.
[86] Ibid., 4.
[87] Ibid., 8.
[88] Ibid., 14-24.
[89] Flory and Miller, 38-39.
[90] Ibid., 39.
[91] Ibid., 82.
[92] Ibid., 162.
[93] Ibid., 162.
[94] Ibid., 163.
[95] Ibid., 171-173.
[96] Colleen Carroll, *The New Faithful: Why Young Adults are Embracing Christian Orthodoxy* (Chicago, IL: Loyola Press, 2002), 13.
[97] Ibid., 52.
[98] Ibid., 89.
[99] Ibid., 94.
[100] Ibid., 95.
[101] Ibid.
[102] Sharon Parks, *Big Questions, Worthy Dreams: Mentoring Young Adults in Their Search for Meaning, Purpose, and Faith* (San Francisco, CA: Jossey-Bass, 2000), 6.
[103] Ibid., 89.
[104] Ibid., 91.
[105] Ibid., 93.
[106] Ibid., 127.
[107] Ibid., 199.
[108] Tom Beaudoin, introduction in *Virtual Faith: The Irreverent Spiritual Quest of Generation X* (San Francisco, CA: Jossey-Bass, 1998), xiii.
[109] Ibid., 88.
[110] Ibid., 89.
[111] Ibid.
[112] Nathan C. Byrd, III, "Narrative Discipleship: Guiding Emerging Adults to 'Connect the Dots' of Life and Faith." *Christian*

Education Journal 8, no. 2 (September 1, 2011): 246. *ATLA Religion Database with ATLASerials*, EBSCO*host* (accessed September 25, 2013).

[113] Ibid., 247.
[114] Ibid., 248.
[115] Ibid.
[116] Ibid., 258.
[117] Thom S. Rainer and Sam S. Rainer, *Essential Church? Reclaiming a Generation of Dropouts* (Nashville, TN: B&H, 2008), 2.
[118] Ibid.
[119] Ibid., 5-6.
[120] Ibid., 7.
[121] Ibid., 22.
[122] Ibid., 27.
[123] Jana L. Sundene and Richard R. Dunn, *Shaping the Journey of Emerging Adults: Life-Giving Rhythms for Spiritual Transformation* (Downers Grove, IL: InterVarsity Press, 2012), 17.
[124] Ibid., 18.
[125] Ibid., 21.
[126] Ibid., 40.
[127] Ibid., 48.
[128] Laurene Beth Bowers, *Designing Contemporary Congregations: Strategies to Attract Those Under Fifty* (Cleveland, OH: Pilgrim Press, 2008), 14.
[129] Ibid.
[130] Ibid.
[131] Ibid., 21.
[132] Ibid., 20.
[133] Ibid., 21.
[134] Ibid.
[135] Ibid., 22.
[136] Donna Thoennes, "Keeping it Real: Research Findings on Authentic Community," *Christian Education Journal* 5, no. 1 (March 1, 2008): 76. *ATLA Religion Database with ATLASerials, EBSCOhost* (accessed September 29, 2013).
[137] Ibid., 80.
[138] Ibid.

[139] Ibid., 82.
[140] Conrad Hackett, "Emerging Adult Participation in Congregations" accessed September 28, 2013, http://www.changingsea.net/essays/ Hackett.pdf.
[141] Ibid., 11.
[142] Penny Edgell, "Faith and Spirituality among Emerging Adults," accessed September 3, 2014, http://doc.wrlc.org/bitstream/handle/2041/122309/Edgell_Faith.pdf?sequence=1.
[143] Ibid., 5.
[144] Annette Mahoney, "Marriage and Family, Faith, and Spirituality among Emerging Adults" accessed September 3, 2014, http://doc.wrlc.org/bitstream/handle/2041/122317/Mahoney_Marriage-Faith.pdf?sequence=1.
[145] Carolyn McNamara Barry, and Stephanie D. Madsen. "Friends and Friendships in Emerging Adulthood." accessed September 3, 2014, http://doc.wrlc.org/bitstream/handle/2041/122313/Barry-Madsen_Friends.pdf?sequence=1.
[146] Ibid., 6.
[147] Ibid., 7.
[148] Gary L. McIntosh, *One Church, Four Generations: Understanding and Reaching All Ages in Your Church* (Grand Rapids, MI: Baker Books, 2002), 122.
[149] Ibid., 136.
[150] Ibid., 139.
[151] Ibid., 137.
[152] Ibid.
[153] Ibid., 146.
[154] Ibid.
[155] Ibid., 139.
[156] Ibid.
[157] Ibid.
[158] Ibid., 140.
[159] Ibid., 141.
[160] Ibid., 145.
[161] Jill Dierberg, and Lynn Schofield Clark, "Media in the Lives of Young Adults: Implications for Religious Organizations" accessed October 28, 2013, http://www.changingsea.net/essays/Dierberg.pdf.

[162] Chris A. Kiesling, "A Long Adolescence in a Lame Direction? What Should We Make of the Changing Structure and Meaning of Young Adulthood?" *Christian Education Journal* 5, no. 1 (March 1, 2008): 17. *ATLA Religion Database with ATLASerials, EBSCOhost* (accessed September 27, 2013).

CHAPTER SIX
THE RECIPE REVEALED

The preceding chapters laid the groundwork for a model of ministry explained and implemented as documented in this chapter. This chapter explains the methodology used in exploring the ingredients necessary for attraction and retention of emerging adults in a model of ministry in order to arrive at a hypothesis for what is necessary to produce this in the larger church. The model began with the belief that by creating a supportive community where preaching, teaching and activities address the holistic concerns of emerging adults will lead to emerging adults to see greater relevance for the church in their lives. However, as discussed later, this belief missed the mark with regard to the data actually collected. This particular study utilized a qualitative methodology. The type of inquiry is phenomenology where Creswell defines phenomenological research as "a strategy of inquiry in which the researcher identifies the essence of human experiences about a phenomenon as described by participants."[1]

Phenomenology is an appropriate strategy to use in the study because relevance it not something that can be quantified. The results of the model will depend on the extent to which participant's feel or sense that the church has become more relevant to them after participating in the model. As part of this, the study will use tools meant to elicit participant descriptions of both the model and their feelings toward the church as a whole and their peers at the conclusion on the study. The expectation is observation of participants as well as direct feedback will support the notion of the phenomenon that continued participation in the model as constructed leads to an increased sense of the church's relevance to the participants. The use of phenomenology will shape the "types of questions asked, the form of data collection, the steps of data analysis, and the final narrative."[2] As a phenomenological study, getting a feel for how participants feel about the community and the church lie at the heart of the design of the questions posed both as part of survey and during the interviews. Specifically, the questions intended to gauge attitudinal change in the participants with regard to the relevance of the church and their need for community.

The Researcher's Role

In failing to make the church relevant for this particular demographic, the context failed to consistently attract emerging adults or retain emerging adults as they enter the range of eighteen to thirty. Navigating the waters of emerging adulthood without a supportive community in churches likely led to bias against the context and bias toward a solution that included community as a focal point. Seminary training led to a more open-minded approach to ministry and therefore a greater kinship with persons who during the years of emerging adulthood wrestle with what they believe and why. In addition, valuing holistic ministry or the approach to ministry that addresses holistic concerns and advocates on behalf of a God believed to be concerned with wholeness in all areas of life adds perspective to the issue of emerging adult attraction and retention. This is also due in part to being an African American who believes God is on the side of the oppressed and that together persons who possess commonalities along the lines of faith and culture can assist each other. Leading the study is a married African American man with a middle class socioeconomic status.

The participants of the study included a majority of persons previously affiliated in the role as a leader of the youth and young adult ministry and persons who had not met prior to the study. In total, ten of seventeen study attendees sat under the past or present leadership of the youth and young adult ministry. These prior and current relationships could have led to a greater probability of their participation in the study. Of the remaining seven, only two of them had prior interactions before the start of the study. Two of these persons married after giving me the privilege of serving as their premarital counselor and officiant for the ceremony. The groom sat under my ministry as part of the youth and young adult ministry during his preteen and teenage years. The last five persons came as the result of personal invitations either from other sources including the previously mentioned persons.

The study is a case of backyard research that introduces several concerns for the study. Normally, this could compromise the data that could be disclosed with the fear of fallout or retribution.[3] However, in this study there exists no such concern regarding disclosure, but such potential issues dictate how that information is disclosed or the names attached to the information. In addition, not currently serving as the pastor presents "difficult power issues" as it relates to having to obtain permission to perform the study and also as it relates to not painting the church in a bad light since due to the pastoral position being held by another. In addition, not serving as the pastor has limited the degree to which absolute honesty and transparency could prevail in those cases where beliefs and positions do not agree with the church's position (since it is the pastor's position). Put another way, in order to avoid controversy and problems within churches, not all complete opinions could be divulged during the model implementation. However, strategies for validity to ensure that the previously mentioned factors do not skew the results include data triangulation which includes not only direct feedback (interviews), but also indirect feedback (observations, unsupervised survey) where participants felt no undue pressure to respond a particular way or were led down a path to a specific answer.

At the contextual level, the study owed its approval to the pastor of the church, the study's gatekeeper, which the study sought prior to model implementation. The pastor granted permission after hearing details concerning the social and religious nature of activities, details concerning the scheduling of the sessions so as not to disrupt previously scheduled events, and details regarding the reporting of the study's findings. Depending upon the leeway afforded to the leadership of emerging adults in a context of implementation by the pastors of these churches, such leaders should likewise secure the necessary approvals even it is limited to making the pastor, church administrator, executive minister, etc. aware of these plans.

Due to the controversial and sensitive nature of the topics discussed, the study established an expectation of confidentiality between all participants including the leader so that outsiders could not link persons' feedback from and comments during the sessions back to particular individuals. Also the study agreed to mask all identities in order to give participants confidence that they could share freely, openly and honestly their beliefs, feelings and attitudes without fear of judgment or repercussions. The retained consent forms signed prior to participation as well as the accompanying information sheets left with participants to keep for their records clearly identified this expectation and protection mechanism.

Purposeful Sampling Strategy

Participants selected for this study currently occupy the demographic of emerging adulthood being between the ages of eighteen and thirty. In addition, participants in the study either held membership in the selected context or participated after accepting an invitation from another participant who holds membership or is at least affiliated with churches. The context selected as the site for this study owed its selection to a number of factors. These factors included that the context lacked a significant emerging adult population. Also, the challenge of attracting and retaining emerging adults is not a new one given the repeated losses of these young adults. Being my home context and spending my emerging adult years in this church added to the rationale for its selection for a study on emerging adult attraction and retention. The study chose these participants and context with the purpose of providing the greatest possible insight into this phenomenon with this demographic in this particular context.

Data Collection Procedures

Emerging adults or young adults between the ages of eighteen and thirty who attended church (not necessarily churches) as well as those who did not served as the actors for the duration of the study. In addition, the events or "what the actors will be observed or interviewed doing" included social activities designed to establish and strengthen the bond of community among the emerging adults along with discussions covering topics relevant to emerging adulthood. The process included the actors determining which games to play and the priority of relevant concerns to discuss. Over the course of the study, the actors took a more active role in the events.

For this study, the "data collection steps include setting the boundaries for the study, collecting information through unstructured or semi structured observations and interviews, documents, and visual materials, as well as establishing the protocol for recording information."[4] With its intent to explore the phenomenon surrounding the implementation of this model, the phenomenological study collected data through observations, interviews, and questionnaires. Only participants who attended at least two of the six sessions during the study received invitations to participate in the post-tests and in-depth interviews in order to truly gauge the impact of the study on the feelings of these participants. The study used these data collection methods to explore subject such as community, relationships, relevance, and the success of the model. Prior to participation in the model, participants signed consent forms and received an information sheet. The Appendix holds copies of each of these forms.

The study collects data through the use of qualitative observations where "the researcher takes field notes on the behavior and activities of individuals at the research site."[5] The study used observations in order to collect unfiltered data that could not otherwise be captured through tests or interviews during the actual model implementation. The study accomplished this collection using the type "observer as participant" allowing for the recording of information "at it occurs" as well as for the recording of information at the conclusion of each service or session.[6] To this end, the study participants heard from the researcher who participated by breaking the ice and doing what was asked of the participants or by starting the various discussions. The observations captured the overall feel of the sessions as well as the audio and visual feedback provided by participants. At the conclusion of each session, an audio file was produced with an oral recollection of the session's events to supplement the notes gathered in an unstructured way during the actual activities of the study. The audio files were produced immediately following each session and received tags with regard to the date of each session. These steps constitute a protocol for recording data from observations which led to an effective capture of both "descriptive" and "reflective notes" of the sessions.[7]

In support of data collection, the study conducted face-to-face, one-on-one interviews with the researcher asking questions of participants who attended more than one session. The study enlisted the use of interviews so that participants would be able to elaborate on feedback provided through the post-test and be able to speak freely with regard to their concerns. Interviews also provided interviewees with the opportunity to give detailed feedback on the effectiveness of the researcher and on the study as a whole to include if the ministry should continue and ways to improve the ministry. The interviews posed five standard open-ended questions coupled with follow-up questions during the interviews. This helped the data by providing additional information, which could not be effectively elicited from the tests or observations. The study utilized an interview protocol which contained each of the elements identified by Creswell to include a heading, instructions, questions, probes for follow-up questions, space between the questions, and a final thank-you statement.[8] The study produced transcripts of these interviews for the purpose of data analysis. Please refer to the Appendix for a sample interview questionnaire as well as a sample transcript.

In reference to questionnaires, the study asked each of its participants to fill out a profile sheet in order to introduce them to the study as well as to use to introduce themselves to each other. The study also posed poll questions to the group to obtain feedback about a number of study related subjects. Survey questions properly formatted to elicit responses where respondents' opinions could range from strongly disagree to strongly agree. The study captured data from both participants and non-participants alike as long as they fell into the definition of the study's actors. The study provided a test to the actors upon their entry into the study and provided a follow up test using the same questions to the actors who actually participated in at least two sessions of the study in order to gauge attitudinal change. The survey ordered the questions to ensure that respondents could not anticipate the next question and mindlessly make their selections without actually reading each question. The measurements targeted in each question therefore varied from question to question. Please see the Appendix for samples of both the profile sheet and the form used for pre- and post-tests.

Data Analysis Steps

The process of data analysis "involves preparing the data for analysis, conducting different analyses, moving deeper and deeper into understanding the data…, representing the data, and making an interpretation of the larger meaning of the data."[9] This is "an ongoing process involving continual reflection about the data, asking analytic questions, and writing memos throughout the study."[10] The analysis also "involves collecting open-ended data, based on asking general questions and developing an analysis from the information supplied by participants."[11] "Basic qualitative analysis" includes collecting qualitative data, analyzing the data for "themes or perspectives," and reporting four to five themes.[12] In the analysis of the data from this phenomenological study, this research "uses the analysis of significant statements, the generation of meaning units, and the development of what Moustakas (1994) calls an essence description."[13]

The general steps of data analysis include organizing the data and preparing it for analysis, reading through the data, coding the data, using the "coding process to generate a description of the setting or people as well as categories or themes for analysis," advancing "how the description and themes will be presented in the qualitative narrative," and "making an interpretation or meaning of the data."[14] The first step of organizing the data includes "transcribing interviews, optically scanning material, typing up field notes, or sorting and arranging the data into different types depending on the sources of information."[15] For the purposes of this study this means organizing the data captured through the use of questionnaires, interviews and observations. The purpose of reading through the data is to "obtain a general sense of the information and to reflect on its overall meaning."[16]

Coding of the data is the "process of organizing the material into chunks or segments of text before bringing meaning to information."[17] For the purposes of this study, this includes "taking text data..., segmenting sentences...into categories, and labeling those categories with a term, often a term based in the actual language of the participant."[18] The description generated in the fourth step "involves a detailed rendering of information about people, places, or events in a setting."[19] Also as part of the fourth step, the research uses the coding to "generate a small number of themes or categories" which "appear as major findings in qualitative studies and are often used to create headings in the findings sections of studies."[20] In this particular phenomenological study, these themes are "shaped into a general description."[21]

Deciding on the presentation of the description and themes could include using a "narrative passage to convey the findings of the analysis."[22] It could also include "visuals, figures, or tables as adjuncts to the discussions."[23] Making an interpretation in the final step of analysis seeks to understand the lessons learned which could include my "personal interpretation, couched in [my] understanding" brought to the study from [my] own culture, history, and experiences."[24] In addition, it could be a "meaning derived from a comparison of the findings with information gleaned from literature or theories" such as the theoretical resources which offer prescriptions for addressing emerging adult attraction and retention. Following this coding activity, with the support of data source triangulation the study will present major findings and conclusions.

Multiple Strategies for Validating the Findings

The study utilizes four strategies for validating the findings and they include credibility, transferability, dependability, and confirmability. In order to establish qualitative validity through credibility, at the conclusion of the study the results and themes will be reviewed with a focus group of participants. This will be with the purpose of ensuring the correctness of my understanding of themes as arisen from their feedback. Also, participants will be polled concerning my understanding of the cultural description formulated through observations. Also, a review of inconsistent or unexpected results between the pre- and post-tests took place in order to validate accuracy for persons who participated in more than two sessions.

The difference between transferability and the researcher's role is that the researcher's role focuses more on the researcher's personal biases independent of the context but transferability focuses on the thorough description of the context and assumptions about the context that went into the research. Over the past twenty years, churches has seen a perpetual pattern where when young adults turn eighteen and no longer have to attend church many of them stop attending. With few exceptions, the church has seen this population dwindle until some of these emerging adults return during their thirties. The context has, at least in the past twenty years, had ministry and programs for the young (under eighteen) and the older and established (thirty and over), but lacked intentional ministry for the emerging adult population. This mass exodus likely finds its genesis in the failure of the context to make church and Christianity sufficiently relevant to persons who become more open-minded to other points of view during the emerging adult years. This study assumed that in failing to make the church relevant for this particular demographic, the context failed to consistently attract emerging adults or retain emerging adults as they enter the range of eighteen to thirty. Going into this study, the belief existed that churches required an intentional effort to address the holistic concerns of emerging adults. Another belief that existed prior to model implementation included the assumption that central to emerging adult attraction and retention laid the establishment of community wherein emerging adults could find a safe space and non-judgmental environment. In summary, the study is transferable specifically to contexts, which lack significant emerging adult presence (i.e. less than ten percent of the membership) and where the context fails to make an intentional effort to make ministry relevant for this demographic.

As the project progressed, different emerging adults began attending. Also, the word began spreading throughout the congregation about the time that the emerging adults had during the sessions. Several people, including those who would not normally converse with me, expressed their pleasure with the project and stated how they thought it was needed in churches and the church at large. Some of the project participants came to church more in the weeks during the duration of the project than they attended the year leading up to the study. A large contingent of the participants returned week after week for each session not wanting to miss any session. Those who missed sessions did so only due to other plans or work plans. Even those who worked beyond the start times of the sessions would immediately come to the session after their shift concluded. During the sessions, participants smiled and expressed their opinions more freely than previously observed and became more vulnerable or trusting as the project continued. The men's ministry in the context of implementation seized upon the success of the model and had their own session over food where they engaged with one another about issues relevant to men. The women's ministry planned, but due to an unanticipated loss, was unable to execute a game night similar to the game nights executed during the model's implementation. The pastor of churches, following the second sermon which covered the New Testament foundation for the model, changed the subject of his daily spiritual text messages to focus on the spirit of community lamented to be absent during the presentation of the sermon. When combined, these facts support the dependability of this project.

To ensure confirmability, the study used three tools for the purpose of data triangulation and they include questionnaires, in-depth interviews, and observations. This study used this triangulation to "build a coherent justification for themes."[25] In addition, a peer associate read the results of the study and agreed with my analysis after giving a cursory view over the raw data. Professional associates also provided feedback and support for the study. Along with this, the inclusion of documented negative instances where feedback diverges from the anticipated outcome also makes the project valid.

Measuring Success

For the purposes of this project, success is defined as arriving at an understanding at the model's conclusion of what ingredients are necessary for a ministry that attracts and retains emerging adults. Data from the three collection methods (observations, questionnaires, and interviews), after analysis, would measure if this definition of success took place during the model in part by measuring attitudinal change. As mentioned above, the major findings presented at the conclusion of analysis will relate to the measurements of relevance and community, and will assist in determining the success of the model based on their ability to lead to a refined hypothesis. As a result of this analysis and major findings, success would also have included creating a repeatable model of ministry for emerging adults based on foundational ingredients although the exact definitions of these ingredients may vary from context to context.

Field Experience

This phenomenological study hypothesized that by creating a supportive community where preaching, teaching and activities address the holistic concerns of emerging adults will lead to emerging adults to see greater relevance for the church in their lives. The purpose of this study was to explore the ingredients necessary for attraction and retention of emerging adults in a model of ministry in order to arrive at a hypothesis for what is necessary to produce this in the larger church. The implementation took place over the course of six weeks with a combination of two sermons designed to shed light on the strategy for the model as well as to inform the congregation about the need of relevant ministry. In addition, the implementation included social events and substantive discussions designed to increase the sense of community and provide relevant ministry for emerging adults. In the space that follows for both sermons and the events held will be described with the date of each being reported. For the sermons, a discussion of the highlights of the sermons as well as observations and feedback follow a general overview. With regard to the events, the philosophy of implementation will be discussed before delving into the details of each session which include the date of meeting, an overview, the purpose, the particular activities followed by observations and outcomes. Designed after intense brainstorming, reflection, and consultation with emerging adults and contextual associates, these events each had specific purpose.

The model began with a sermon that used the Old Testament scripture as a foundation. Since the beginning of the model included a biblically based discussion, it was determined that the next event should be mostly a social event with the aim of introducing participants to the model and fostering community. Then it seemed fitting to follow this session with the first of two sessions, which discussed biblical perspectives on relevant topics. The model placed the third session, "Sharing Our Stories" next in line again for the purpose of building community and creating a connection between the participants. The second session discussing biblical perspectives on relevant topics followed before the presentation of the second sermon that focused on the New Testament foundation. The following week offered another game night. The final session elicited feedback from participants and helped determine a way forward while also providing the ability for participants to remain in contact. In general, it was determined that the best course of action was to alternate social and biblical sessions so as to provide balance.

With the permission of the pastor of churches, each sermon was preached during the 11:20 am service on the second Sunday during the months of implementation, which serves as the Youth and Young Adult Ministry emphasis Sunday. The model selected this time due to the belief that this service would have the highest number of emerging adults based on previous observation. Each sermon was preached with the help of a tablet, used in this way for the first time, as opposed to a paper manuscript for the purpose of using relevant means to present the relevant message.

The study began with the preaching of the Old Testament foundation found in Second Chronicles 30:1-13, 21-27 on February 9, 2014. However, for the purpose of time the preached passage only included Second Chronicles 30:1, 10-13, 21-23. The sermon was titled "An Invitation Worth Accepting." The sermon introduced the theme by discussing the various forms of invitations and stated that the text served as a model for church growth and personal evangelism. The points of emphasis included the nature of the invitation, the result of the invitation, and the benefit from accepting the invitation. The nature of the invitation covered the inviter's identity, integrity, motive, method and relevant message. The result of the invitation discussed the potential acceptance or rejection of the invitation to salvation and Christian community. The benefit from accepting the invitation included the fact that the members of the community received what they needed, which included an experience that they did not want to end. The sermon then concluded with a discussion of how Christians accepted God's invitation to salvation and how Jesus accepted the invitation to redeem humankind. Also, in order to make the invitation to Christian discipleship more relevant, its nature was thoroughly explained. The sermon raised the names of these contextual associates during the sermon for the purpose of encouraging them not to give up even in the face of rejection as experienced by Hezekiah's messengers.

The second sermon in the study took place on March 9, 2014 with a sermon entitled "Relevant Ministry Makes the Difference." The selected passage for this sermon had its roots in the New Testament foundation for the model but for this purpose only included Acts 2:14, 29-32, 41-47. This sermon introduced the theme defining relevance, discussing the struggle to find relevance and the need for relevant ministry. The points of emphasis in this sermon included the fact that relevant ministry that makes a difference includes relevant preaching and a community that matters. With regard to the issue of relevant preaching, the sermon argued that when it comes to relevant preaching any Christian can participate, it must be relevant to the preacher (proclaimer), it must be relevant to its audience, and that it produces fruit. When it came to the relevant community that matters, the sermon began by discussing the model's historical foundation found in the life and community of Perpetua. The sermon argued that relevant community includes people with whom Christians have something in common, helps Christians continue in the faith, serves as a supportive community, and leads to results. The sermon concluded by exalting Jesus as the epitome of a preacher with a relevant message who showed that community mattered and made the greatest difference of all. Months after this sermon's presentation, the pastor of churches still referred back to it and publicly talked about how the sermon encouraged him and led him to strive to be more relevant in his preaching.

Outside of the sermons, the model included six continuous weeks of meeting every Saturday evening at five o'clock in the church's fellowship hall. Each of these sessions started about forty-five minutes later than scheduled due to waiting on participants to arrive. However, each of these sessions lasted from two to three hours as the participants seemed to not want to leave. Tables were arranged and surrounded by chairs in order to give the feel of a roundtable meeting so that each participant could see each other and maintain eye contact especially in moments of sharing. The contextual associates helped to determine the timing for the events, Saturdays at five o'clock, based on work schedules and the flexibility it offered for their social events both before and after each session. The menu was chosen based on known elements of the young adult diet from previous experience. The session where participants shared their stories was the only session for which the menu was not predetermined, but depended upon the participants. The model advertised the events in a number of ways to include word of mouth, flyers, text messaging, personal calls, and social media including Twitter, Facebook and Instagram. In order to provide incentive for attendance, each event included food. As noted previously, the events included a meet, greet and game night, two sessions on biblical perspectives on relevant topics, a session entitled "Sharing Our Stories," another game night, and a wrap-up session.

On February 15, 2014 the Meet, Greet and Game Night took place and the participants filled out paperwork to include consent forms, a profile questionnaire, and an initial survey. The participants then heard of the overall purpose of the model and the hopeful outcome of the sermons and sessions. The study included this particular event with the purpose of building community by encouraging interpersonal dialogue, discussion of vulnerability, and by having fun together as a group. Each emerging adult was responsible for answering questions from the profile sheet (see Appendix A) and using their answers to introduce themselves to everyone else. Following each person's introduction, the session paired off the participants who then discussed their commonalities. At the conclusion of this activity, the participants played team games including Family Feud. Then one group of four broke off to play the game of Spades while the rest played a game called Logos. Even though many of the participants knew each other, sharing the answers to those questions and having dialogue in pairs allowed them to see each other in a new light as they learned new things about each other.

The study held the first of two sessions covering biblical perspectives on relevant topics on February 22, 2014. The original plan was to go through the Bible and present different stories showing them the relevance of the story to their lives as young adults. The original plan also included the notion of having the four emerging adult contextual associates to highlight some biblical story from which they extracted relevant information to their lives as young adults. After consultation with a cousin, the design for the session evolved into one that would introduce the Bible before offering biblical perspectives on relevant topics, which the participants chose and prioritized. Specifically, this session included a discussion of the purpose and background of the Bible. Then the model established a protocol for these topics where the topic would be defined, the biblical perspective given and then the floor would be opened for discussion. This laid the foundation to discuss relevant topics for emerging adults, and the topics discussed as part of this session included sex, homosexuality and appropriate dress. This session sought to show that the Bible could be relevant while bringing them together as a community in a safe space for them to discuss relevant issues. Once again the session provided refreshments for the participants in the form of sandwich trays, chips, and drink.

The study continued with a session entitled "Sharing Our Stories" on March 1, 2014 with the purpose of creating a greater sense of community by having participants share about past triumphs, present struggles and future endeavors. The reasoning for this session included the belief that by opening up to each other and sharing difficulties and stories of overcoming participants would forge a stronger connection and support one another. As part of this session, the study asked each participant to bring a dish which had a story attached. Leadership broke the ice in sharing stories after which participants shared their stories. The reasons given by participants for their bringing of various dishes included the fact that some were favorite dishes and the rest somehow involved family.

The study held the second session on biblical perspectives on relevant topics March 8, 2014. The original designed called for strictly a rap session where they got to talk about various issues but was replaced based on the success of the first biblical perspectives session and participants' desire to continue talking about relevant topics. This session shared its purpose with the first session. Once again participants voted on the topics to discuss and they decided to discuss friendship, dating, suffering, drugs and alcohol. The next week's session included another game night held on March 15, 2014 with more team games such as Family Feud and Taboo. The purpose of this night was to have fun and increase the sense of community between the participants.

The last session of the study occurred on March 22, 2014 with the purpose of receiving feedback from participants and obtaining their reflections on what took place. In addition, the particular activities included posing poll questions and giving participants the opportunity to vent and express whatever was on their mind at the time. In addition, the study conducted interviews, discussed ways to improve the ministry, and collected data from post-tests. The combination of the sermons and social events effectively ministered to the young adults. The sermons and the events received positive feedback from observers and participants alike. Approximately five weeks after the final study meeting, the group reconvened and welcomed three new participants to the group.

Data Results

Observations

The first sermon experience began the model of ministry and provided a unique perspective from which to observe. All but one of the contextual associates attended this first sermon. The sermon managed to hold the attention of people in the congregation even garnering laughter and positive witnessing by expressed "amen." During the sermon and after its conclusion persons approved of its content noting the particular points of the sermon that resonated with them. For example, the discussion of Hezekiah's age, integrity, and use of media relevant to his context made an impact. Many spoke in glowing terms about the sermon's presentation as well as the necessity and relevance of the message using terms such as relevant, needed, strong, and important. At the conclusion of the sermon, several persons confirmed their intentions to attend the model's sessions.

The first model session began forty-five minutes late with a description of the model after the arrival of the session's ten participants. Attendees agreed with the diagnosis concerning the church's attraction and retention of emerging adults to the point that they discussed leaving churches in search of relevant ministry. After filling out profile sheets, and other necessary model paperwork, participants openly shared the content of their profile sheets and personal information with each other both in a group setting as well as in pairs. This exchange exposed their shared interest in discussing homosexuality and other topics already slated for discussion in the following session. Sharing in this way gave attendees an opportunity to observe commonality and to connect. For a sample profile sheet, please see Appendix A. The emerging adults provided positive final feedback, such as the comments that these types of sessions were relevant while also lamenting the lack of relevant activities for emerging adults at this session's conclusion after playing competitive games.

The second session addressed relevant topics from a biblical perspective where discussion on sex, homosexuality, and proper dress followed an introduction to the Bible. In spite of the controversial nature of these topics, participants agreed on the order in which to discuss them before freely and honestly commenting on each topic. During the discussions, attendees asked about a number of things to include masturbation and pornography. The emerging adults provided only positive feedback about the handling of these topics and the session even commenting that it was relevant, should continue beyond the six weeks and that it was necessary. While certain participants expressed frustration with how they are treated as compared to others in churches, another reported that the session helped her, as a homosexual, by discussing how the church should treat those with alternative lifestyles in which the church and the Bible appear to disagree. This session seemed to exceed both emerging adult expectations with regard to its relevance and perspective.

During the third session, attendees shared past triumphs, present obstacles yet to be overcome and anticipated future victories. Participants paid attention as their peers spoke about overcoming past shortcomings and hurts, struggling in their present with personal challenges (i.e. single parenting, career obstacles, low self-esteem and smoking marijuana), and achieving successful careers in the future (i.e. nurse practitioner, producer, and a chef). To go with this, upon invitation participants brought dishes to which a story was to be attached and each of the stories provided dealt with some aspect of community or family. Without exception, the participants remained open, honest, and transparent about their struggles after leadership broke the ice.

Similarly to the second session, the fourth session provided an opportunity for eight emerging adults present to discuss biblical perspectives on relevant topics. For different reasons, two first-time attendees departed the session early. The first departed before the session's start due to anxiety brought on by being in the presence of the father of her daughter (Participant Five). This reflects the fact that one of the challenges to creating community among emerging adults is the presence of prior complex relationships between those attempting to participate in the community. The second departed due to other plans, but enjoyed the session after participating openly and thoroughly. In this session, participants chose to discuss marriage, drugs, alcohol and suffering. The session also broached the topic of technology in the church. Sessions like this one gave rise to the same type of session for the Men's Ministry at churches where food accompanies conversation on relevant topics.

The second sermon of the model grabbed everyone's attention, including the young adults, and everyone seemed to enjoy the message. Several things stood out for the congregation and these

THE RECIPE REVEALED 143

include points related to prayer, community, and the relevance of the gospel. Observed were the congregation's "winces, oohs and aahs" during the parts of the sermon where hard truths were presented such as the fact that the spirit of community has vacated many churches. This sermon also received positive feedback with regard to sermon content (i.e. relevant and very good) and its good presentation (i.e. passionate and good rhythm). Some of the sessions' participants attended this sermon. The sermon's focus on relevant ministry and community seemingly moved the pastor to focus more on relevant ministry and community based on his words and actions.

A game night with a relevant menu constituted the activity of the fifth session. In the midst of playing Family Feud and Taboo participants laughed a great deal and enjoyed the food thoroughly. For this session a few new persons attended who were friends of persons who had already attended a number of sessions. A few of the persons arrived after leaving the places where they had other plans. The session lasted three hours as, once again, as Hezekiah observed, the participants had such a great time that they were not in a hurry to go home. This session also lasted about three hours. At its conclusion, several persons spoke of how they wanted to see this ministry continue. Participant Eight, because it was the last session she could attend, lamented to the others that she hoped that she would see them again. As with the Men's Ministry, the Women's Ministry mimicked the activities of the project by scheduling a game night only after observing or hearing about the success of the emerging adults' game night.

The sixth and final session provided the emerging adults present with an opportunity to vent, but surprisingly they did not have much about which they desired to vent. During a recap of the model's activities, participants agreed with the need for relevance, and another revealed that tips for biblical interpretation stayed with him. In addition, attendees provided positive feedback on the model (i.e. with regard to the creation of community) and feedback concerning additional topics to discuss that included world affairs and finance. The group also voiced concerns about confidentiality and leadership before offering suggestions for improving the ministry. These suggestions centered on what they believed to be necessary to ensure relevant community. This included being separated from the youth (with the exception of older teenagers) in the church rather than being lumped in with them under the same ministry umbrella.

The model also made observations with regard to the success of the model attracting and retaining emerging adults based on attendance. The model successfully attracted twenty-one participants who in responding to questionnaires provided data for analysis. Only seventeen of these emerging adults attended at least one session. In addition, on average these twenty-one participants attended 2.14 sessions. However, of those who attended at least one session the average number of sessions attended was a little more than two and a half sessions at 2.65 sessions. Seventeen of the twenty-one data participants participated in at least one session. Of these, more than half attended three sessions or more. The remainder of respondents only participated in one session each largely due to scheduling conflicts. Only one of the identified emerging adult contextual associates for the model failed to attend a single session due to her work schedule, yet she was present for each of the model's sermons. The remaining emerging adult contextual associates attended an average of three sessions. The model only invited individuals who attended at least two of the non-sermonic sessions to participate in the post-test and in-depth interviews. On average, participants in the focus group attended 4.125 sessions each. Please reference Appendix E for tables and figures pursuant to participant attendance.

Questionnaires
Participants

In total, twenty-one emerging adults between the ages of eighteen and thirty participated in the initial set of questionnaires and tests. The average age of these respondents was 22.2 which closely reflected the median age of twenty-two. Of these twenty-one persons, males constituted 38.1% of the group with the other 61.9% comprised of females. With the exception of one Caucasian and one Hispanic participant, the rest of the model participants were African American. Of the twenty-one persons who filled out profile sheets only 19.05 were married with the other 80.95 being single. As mentioned previously, only those individuals who attended at least two sessions received invitations to complete the post-test and interviews. While nine of the initial twenty-one participants fit this criteria, only eight participated in the post-tests with seven of these also going on to participate in the in-depth interviews. Each of the profiles for the focus group participants documented in Table 2 of Appendix E reflects personal information that was true about the participants at the time of data collection. The profiles for each member of the focus group, which are almost all African American with a Hispanic exception, include an alias, age, gender, marital status, whether the member is a parent, whether the individual served as a context associate, and the number of sessions that he or she attended prior to the conclusion of the model. The focus group participants possessed diversity with regard to age and marital status, but were evenly split with regard to gender with half of the focus group being male and the other half female. The average age and median age of this group were both twenty-three with the youngest being nineteen and the oldest twenty-seven (see Figure 5.1 for a graph of the focus group age distribution). The highest number of sessions attended for a person in this group was six while the lowest number of sessions attended was three (see Figure 5.2 for a graph of the focus group session attendance).

Profile Sheets

Each participant responded to a questionnaire entitled "Getting to Know You…" (see Appendix A for a sample). This section summarizes the responses given by all twenty-one participants on a question-by-question basis. Respondents revealed a number of things about themselves on these sheets that they then shared with the community. Community bears importance to them as evidenced by the fact that nearly all respondents experienced community in their families and through social media (i.e. Facebook and Twitter). Furthermore, they revealed that they were in the process of positioning themselves in the present for where they saw themselves ten years from when the model collected this data. For example, many worked and or attended school at model time while anticipated successful careers and stable finances ten years from the model implementation time. The emerging adults who took part provided a plethora of adjectives for how they describe themselves including open-minded, intelligent and friendly, just to name a few. They offered varied responses with regard to the issues that they would like to see addressed in churches to include hypocrisy and relationships. For further detail concerning the feedback provided on this tool concerning topics for which participants expressed a desire to discuss, please consult Appendix E. The model anticipated some of these but used the feedback from this questionnaire the second and fourth model sessions. Also, participants gave answers of the arts and family, among other things, in response to a question about their passion while their responses for favorite musical artist, sport and food varied. Similarly, the emerging adults mentioned a number of activities in which they participate for fun including exercising and spending time with family. This data captured using this tool demonstrated that emerging adults are not a monolithic group with all the same tastes and preferences. The model asked these questions as a means to create room for common ground with other respondents to facilitate the creation of community when sharing their responses.

Poll Questions

The model also used poll questions throughout implementation in order to gauge the opinions of participants. Participants responded to a number of these questions at the first model session and during the final session. During the first session attendees unanimously agreed on a number of statements including the statements that the church should address holistic issues, that older people in the church would keep them or have kept them from being involved in the church, that the emerging adult period of their lives is important to the rest of their lives, and that they had friends who did not attend church because they did not find it relevant. However, they were split on the subject of leaving their churches when given as some expressed agreement while others disagreed. At the end of the model, emerging adults present responded unanimously in agreement with the statements that the project helped them see that church can be relevant, that they would like to continue in a ministry such as this, and that they met people during the project with which they would like to remain connected.

Pre-Test Results

In support of this model, as previously mentioned, twenty-one emerging adults between the ages of eighteen and thirty responded to the test provided to all respondents prior to their participation in this model. The test utilized a likability scale for eighteen statements (a sample of the test can be found in Appendix B). To view a figure presenting the outcome of the pre-test, please refer to Appendix E. For the purpose of analysis, this discussion groups together the statements meant to test for similar measurements. For example, Statements one, three, seven, eleven, twelve, fourteen and fifteen test on the subject of relevance or meaning while the rest of the statements focus on the subject of community with the exceptions of Statements four and five test on the subject of both relevance and community.

Overall, the feedback from the statements concerning relevance paints a somewhat contradictory picture. For example, a strong majority of respondents agreed that the church and Christian faith had relevance. At the same time, 24.5% of participants provided little hope by agreeing that churches are not capable of making the church and Bible relevant to young adults. Participants also suggested a divergence from God and the church by agreeing that God cared about their whole lives while disagreeing with the notion that the church addresses all of their concerns. In addition, the emerging adults responded nearly unanimously in agreeing that they encountered someone or a ministry that dealt with what bore importance to them. With regard to Statements four and five that specifically address the relevance of the church, eighteen of the twenty-one respondents agreed or strongly agreed that having a community of young adults makes the church feel more relevant. This same number of respondents also agreed or strongly agreed that having persons of similar background and age to talk to helps them to see the relevance of the church.

The feedback on the statements focusing on the theme of community is similarly complex. These statements deal with not only the respondent's location within a supportive community, but also with their perceived need for such community. Test respondents nearly unanimously stated that they have supportive and encouraging people in their lives with whom they can work out their feelings and beliefs. Also, the majority believed in the importance of having a support system for their Christian journeys. Similarly, a strong majority expressed that they could see the point of getting together with other Christians demonstrating the importance to them of having a community consisting of peers. However, a majority of respondents in a sense confirmed the absence of community in their churches. As a result, it appeared that while community was important the churches of participants failed to supply community for emerging adults.

On the other hand, participants reported not feeling lonely, isolated or alone, but rather connected with people who could help them in their Christian journeys. This makes sense considering that a strong majority believed that they needed other's help in their journey and they needed people around them to encourage them to do the right thing and please God. That said, less than half could agree to have found a safe space conducive to free speech and free of judgment. Overall, it appeared to them that community is necessary, but always supplied in the church. These facts seem to underscore the idea that being a part of a community of their peers is important to emerging adults. As a result, it appears that while community is important community is not necessarily being supplied in their churches to include churches. Overall, respondents seemed to communicate that community is necessary, but not always provided or nourished within the church.

Focus Group Results

As noted above, the model only invited only participants in the model's activities who attended at least two sessions to participate in post-tests as well as in-depth interviews. While nine participants fit these parameters for consideration, only eight of them took part in post-tests. The space that follows discusses the pre-test results for this select group of respondents followed by a discussion surrounding the post-tests results for the same focus group. Consideration will be given to the meaning of attitudinal change as observed by contrasting the pre-test and post-test data. In the spirit of qualitative research, each of the questions for the pre-test and post-test are exactly the same as listed in Table 1 in Appendix E. Appendix E contains figures that graph the results for the data provided by the participants of emphasis. For the sake of clarity and consistency, the space below presents the data in an order similar to that used for discussing the pre-test results above.

With regard to Statement one, there existed no notable change in attitude as the same 75% of respondents agreed or strongly agreed that church is relevant to their lives before and after their participation in the model. While encouraging on one hand, the model's failure to help one participant agree with this sentiment is disappointing. In similar fashion, 62.5% of respondents agreed or strongly agreed both before and after the model that they could see the relevance of the Christian faith to their lives as young adults (Statement Three).

Unexpectedly, some of the results diverge from the intended results. For example, after the model 50% of respondents as compared with 25% before the model stated that they agreed or strongly agreed that churches are not capable of making the church and the Bible relevant to young adults (Statement Seven). This data point seems to suggest that the model had the reverse intended effect, at least on this particular question. At the same time, 12.5% more of respondents grew to disagree or strongly disagree that the church addresses all of their concerns. In addition, to Statement Twelve, after the model the data shows an increase of 12.5% in the number of focus group participants who agreed or strongly agreed they had not encountered anyone or any ministry that deals with what's important to them. Conversely, on the same question, the data reflects a 12.5% increase in the number of persons who said that they had encountered someone or some ministry that deals with what's important to them.

However, in an encouraging turn of events the responses to Statement Fourteen demonstrate expected attitudinal change at 15%. In the case of Statement Fourteen, after the model 87.5% of respondents strongly agreed that God cared about their whole lives and not simply their spiritual parts as compared with 75% who agreed or strongly agreed with this notion pre-model. For Statement Fifteen, 87.5% of respondents came to agree or strongly agree that the Bible has principles and stories that are applicable to their lives in contradistinction to the 75% of participants who felt this way prior to their participation in this model. On the whole, the data suggests a mixed result with some attitudes remaining the same, some diverging from expectations, some aligning with expectations, and one with a mix of both encouraging and discouraging data with regard to the model and its effect on the perception of the relevance of church to respondents.

When it comes to the statements on the tests that primarily addressed the theme of community, the overall picture in terms of attitudinal change is positive. On Statement Two, after the implementation of the model 100% of participants agreed or strongly agreed that they had people in their lives who will support and encourage them and with whom they could work out their feelings and beliefs. More positive attitudinal change arises from taking a look at the data where 100% of respondents after the model as compared with 87.5% of respondents after the model agreed or strongly agreed that having people in their lives that will support them in their Christian journeys was important. In a similar vein, compared with 75% of respondents pre-model, 100% of respondents agreed or strongly agreed that they could see the point of getting together with other young adult Christians post-model. Each of these three results represents positive and anticipated attitudinal change with regard to how they saw community.

However, contrary to this positive news, the feedback received for Statements Nine and Ten present a mixed bag. For the former, at the conclusion of the model 37.5% of respondents believed that community was absent from their church in contradistinction to the 25% who believed this before their participation in the model. When it comes to Statement Ten, on a negative note one person then believed at the conclusion of the model that they felt lonely, isolated or alone in their journey when no persons felt this way prior to the model. On the other hand, on this same statement, 62.5% of participants disagreed or strongly disagreed with this sentiment before the sessions as compared with 75% who believed so after the model.

While some of the data concerning Statements Nine and Ten were disappointing, some news of attitudinal change in the direction of expected results took place. Largely, at the termination of the model's sessions, respondents exhibited an attitudinal change consistent with expectations as evidenced by their responses to Statements Thirteen, Sixteen, Seventeen and Eighteen. On Statement Thirteen, the portion of respondents who agreed or strongly agreed that they sensed connections to people who they knew could help them in their journey as a Christian grew from 75% to 87.5%. In a similar way, on Statement Sixteen, at the end of the model 100% of test participants agreed or strongly agreed that they needed people around them who would encourage them to do the right thing and please God as contrasted with 75% before the model began. Also, whereas 75% of respondents agreed or strongly agreed that they needed others' help in their journey before the model, 87.5% believed this at the model's conclusion. On the subject of Statement Eighteen, 75% of persons tested agreed or strongly agreed that in the church of implementation they found a safe space where they could speak freely and not be judged.

When it came to the statements on the test that touched on the themes of relevance and community, the results were similarly positive. On Statement Four, before and after the model 75% of participants agreed or strongly agreed that having a community of young adults makes the church feel more relevant. While this did not show attitudinal change toward the expected outcome, keeping this number steady was a positive development. Also, after terminating model activities, 87.5% of respondents came to agree or strongly agree that having persons of similar background and age to talk to helps them see the relevance of the church as compared with 75% before model activities began. This data point reflects a movement in attitudinal change toward the expected results. In the additional comments Participants Seven and Eight provided positive feedback. Participant Seven reported that before this model took place she "felt some type of way about [context] and truly finding a new worship home." Participant Eight added that this model should be kept up and that she enjoyed it. She also reflected positively on her chance to meet new people with whom she shared common ground and from whom she could hear different perspectives. Overall, the results from the post-tests support the idea that the model's activity contributed to an attitudinal change consistent with expectations on the measurements of relevance and community.

Interview Results

The model utilized interviews as a third method of data collection. The space that follows describes the feedback received from members of the focus group as identified above—those persons who attended at least two sessions. For the purpose of analysis, the project grouped the interview questions and answers based on the nature of the question. Specifically, the analysis grouped together open-ended questions on one hand and questions that expected yes or no responses along with clarifications on the other. The space below presents the data collected from the open-ended questions prior to examining the results of the remaining questions.

Responses to the open-ended questions yielded quality feedback from those interviewed. When asked how they felt about the project, participants responded with a positive view of the project and their feedback included adjectives such as relevant, necessary, helpful, and informing. In addition, some spoke positively about meeting new people with whom they had things in common and from people who shared their perspectives openly. Similarly, respondents only used positive adjectives to describe their experience in the project to include openness, a community of peers, and expressing their desire for the model to continue beyond the scheduled six weeks. At the same time, respondents reported that the best part of the model activities had to do with the openness of participants who participated in a non-judgmental and supportive community of their peers. To this point, Participant Four noted that the best part was getting some acknowledgement that he was not the only one having a rough time in life. With regard to their descriptions of the sense of community, interviewees reported that it was a non-judgmental and supportive community characterized by a spirit of openness where they discussed relevant topics with Participant One noting that there was a "strong sense of community."

Along the same lines, when probed concerning whether or not the community was supportive or judgmental, every emerging adult interviewed reported that it was supportive and non-judgmental enabling the freedom to be open. When provided with an opportunity to provide feedback concerning the leadership of the group, several participants applauded that because of this leadership conversations flowed while staying on task without feeling controlled. Overall, on this question, interviewees lauded the openness and flexibility of leadership as well as the success in getting people to come. The project was impactful in discussing relevant topics as well as the fact that it aided personal development and led to retention for Participant Two at the church as the result of this ministry.

However, when asked about the impact participants foresaw after implementing this project at this church or elsewhere the responses were positive, but varied. These responses included the predicted attraction of youth and young adults as well as personal development to include a better lifestyle or resisting temptation. Apparently, this project's implementation at churches or elsewhere, in the opinion of Participant Two, would lead to an increased sense of relevance. Participant Two also noted that such activities including socializing and learning resonates with young people. Participants mentioned getting more people in response to a question asking how to improve the model or in what ways could the project have been better. In this way, they lamented the failure of the model to attract more persons. To this end, when asked for methods on how to attract more people some participants acknowledged the relevance of the methods used before mentioning word of mouth and social media as means to attract more emerging adults.

Responses to questions that expected yes or no responses along with clarifications also yielded a wealth of information concerning the effectiveness of the model and insight into the beliefs of emerging adults. Every member of the focus group reported that the project helped him or her to see the relevance of the church. Reasons for this stance included the presence of a community consisting of peers and that the model brought to light previously unanswered questions. When asked about the importance of relevance for attracting and retaining young adults once again respondents unanimously agreed to its importance. In support of this, Participant Two noted that the church need to have something to which the youth can relate and

Participant Four replied that a failure to make the church relevant for emerging adults could have consequences for later generations. Participant Five added that the church has to make it relevant to bring people in while Participant Six highlighted the need for relevant issues in emerging adult attraction and retention. On a related note, respondents agreed that they discussed relevant issues and this made the church feel more relevant so much so that Participant Two no longer saw a need to leave churches.

Of those who responded to the question of whether or not the activities helped them, each responded yes crediting the openness among the participants as well has discussing relevant topics. Also, everyone who responded felt as if they found a community that had a safe space with people whom they could be honest and share their stories because of the openness of participants and their ability to get along with each other. Furthermore, the majority of participants believed that being in community with their peers made it more likely for them to remain in the church with only one person remaining neutral. For those who believed this, they spoke of its ability to retain persons in particular while giving credit to the ability to openly discuss relevant issues in a non-judgmental community of their peers. Similarly, only Participant Two responded neutrally on the question of whether or not they met people that can help them reach their dreams and become better Christians due to a supportive community characterized by openness.

According to the data collected, all but one of those interviewed met people with whom they desired to remain connected. However, they unanimously agreed that sharing their stories made them feel more connected to other participants due to the openness of their peers in that community. Also, in unanimous fashion participants agreed that the leader was transparent and willing to take on controversial subjects, and that doing so made the experience feel more relevant. For example, Participant Two noted the impossibility of reaching emerging adults without honesty about the mistakes of leadership even stating that there is no point to being in leadership if those you lead do not feel comfortable speaking to the leader or asking the leader for guidance. Others noted that such transparency humanizes leadership, shows that leadership cares, and that it brings leadership down to the people who may agree with Participant Three who alluded to transparency's ability to build trust.

Data collected with regard to the question of the model's effect on giving participants a greater chance to remain faithful was more mixed only because while the majority agreed, two persons believed that their faith remained stable and unaffected in a negative way due to the model. Of those who agreed, they praised the openness with which they discussed relevant issues in a non-judgmental and supportive community of their peers for this increased chance. More decisively was the data in regard to this ministry attracting participants in churches or another church with the only Participant Five remaining neutral in reporting that knowing persons at a church is more important. Participant Two noted that having a non-judgmental community helps and each of those who responded reported that having such a ministry increases the chances that they would stay around.

Interviewees unanimously agreed that the ministry should continue in part because it is necessary and could attract young adults as it provides a place where participants can be open. In addition, those who responded to the question of whether or not they would continue attending each replied yes and this demonstrated the model's ability to retain. On the final interview question, respondents agreed to the relevant nature of the methods used to advertise the events including social media, word of mouth, and text messaging. Participant Seven also mentioned how social media provided a platform for community without having to be in the church. She stated this in response to every participant chiming in to encourage a fellow participant in her effort to pass a nursing exam and to every participant returning to the Facebook thread to congratulate her after she informed everyone that she passed. This facilitated, to Participant Seven, a supportive community. Each of the data collection methods yielded a wealth of information. The next section discusses the results of the analysis of this data through the use of codes or categories.

Data Analysis

Coding Results

The model utilized the analysis of the data as mentioned above through the use of coding to arrive at a list of categories for data collected from model participants. After examination of the data, the four major categories of relevance, community, openness, and model effectiveness emerged above the rest. Each of these categories also had subcategories that this work describes below. For each category or subcategory, this space then revisits excerpts to provide examples of data that fit into these categories or subcategories.

To begin, each of the tools utilized in the study contained data related to the major category of relevance. In this vein, several pieces of data fell into the subcategories of relevant issues, relevance as the result of holding emerging adults' attention, the relevance of the church, the relevance of technology, and the lamentation of relevant ministry for emerging adults. An example of data that fit into the subcategory of relevant issues came in the form of interview data on the part of Participant Five who stated that the project addressed some of the things that he desired to discuss but does not hear discussed in church. At the same time, the observation of people being engaged and young adults paying attention during the sermon fit into the subcategory of holding emerging adults' attention. The focus group results that showed that 75% of respondents agreed that church is relevant to their lives fit into the subcategory of the relevance of the church. For the subcategory of relevant technology, a sample of data that fit into this category includes the observation of a member of the congregation agreeing that the church should use technology relevant to the present. Also, the report that emerging adults have to travel a long way to find relevant ministry observed at the end of one of the sessions fits into the subcategory of the lamentation of relevant ministry for emerging adults.

Continuing with these categories it should also be noted that each method of collection led to the collection of data that fit into the major category of community. Under this major category laid the subcategories of nonjudgmental community, supportive community, a community that gets along, social media, and a community of peers. For example, the fact that 75% of participants tested after the model agreed that they found a safe space where they could speak freely and not be judged fits into the subcategory of a nonjudgmental community. Along the same lines, the data collected in interviews with each participant agreeing to the supportive nature of the community falls into the subcategory of supportive community. Participant Five's feedback during his interview where he stated that everybody seemed to get along exemplifies the category of a community where members of the community got along. In addition, data from the profile sheets that demonstrated emerging adult participation in social media finds a home in the subcategory of social media. Finally, for this code of community, the observation that during the first session emerging adults had a great deal of commonality with regard to their families of origin, activities in which they participate for fun, and their age range.

Also, the model collected data that demonstrated the category or theme of openness. This major category gave rise to the subcategories of openness on the part of the leader, openness on the part of participants, and openness protected with confidentiality. For example, the agreement on the part of respondents in interviews that transparent leadership and a willingness to be open and honest on the part of leadership made the experience feel more relevant as leadership tackled controversial subjects would fall into the subcategory of openness on the part of the leader. For the second subcategory of participant openness, the observation that participants talked among themselves openly about a desire to leave their church or their sharing of embarrassing facts from their profile sheets fit. With regard to the final subcategory of openness protected with confidentiality, Participant Three's statement of the importance of confidentiality supports the subcategory of openness protected with confidentiality. In the end, the major codes through the use of these subcategories find sufficient support from each of the data collection methods.

The final major category of data includes data that was related to model effectiveness. This category includes subcategories of emerging adult attraction and retention in or as a result of the model, data that indicated a desire to continue sessions, and data that reflected a desire to continue the model of ministry beyond its six-week scope. The first subcategory of emerging adult attraction and retention in or as a result of the model finds support in the observations of emerging adult attraction and retention based on attendance records. For example, twenty-one emerging adults participated with the majority of them also attending at least one session while another indicated the model's effectiveness in keeping her at churches. At the same time, emerging adults did not seem to want to leave, but desired to extend their time in the model's sessions even seeming disappointed that the final session ended early. Also, undergirding the subcategory of the desire to continue the model beyond its six-week scope were comments on multiple occasions from emerging adult participants stating that they desired for the model to continue beyond the six weeks or that the model should keep going. The model collected such feedback from observations, from the response to a poll question on the subject, and focus group member's responses to interviews.

Major Findings

At the conclusion of the model of ministry, the study identified four major findings after an analysis of the data collected. The study found that a ministry geared toward emerging adult attraction and retention should include relevant content, community, openness, and a design similar to the model of ministry. For each of these ingredients, this space utilizes data collected from observations, questionnaires, and interviews to support the arrival at these major findings. More specifically, several pieces of data from each source of data undergird each of these conclusions in the order of the data collected by observations, questionnaires, and interviews.

To begin, the model found that relevant content evidenced by addressing relevant issues and utilizing technology is necessary for emerging adult ministry. The finding of the necessity of relevant content finds support in each of the three tools each of which led to evidence of the need for discussing relevant issues as well as making the church relevant. First, the observations recorded during the study support this finding for the necessity of relevance. The observations recorded report that some persons noted that ministry needs to be relevant to reach people and young people in particular, and that the attendees participated openly when discussing relevant topics such as homosexuality and sex among other things. Also, data from the questionnaires also supports this finding. After the model, 87.5% of respondents agreed that God cared about their whole lives and not just their spiritual parts while 87.5% of participants also agreed that the Bible has principles and stories that are applicable to their lives. Each of these figures represents attitudinal change and reflects the positive impact of the model on participants. Along similar lines, respondents unanimously agreed that the church should address holistic issues and freely provided relevant issues they desired to discuss.

The data collected as the result of interviews with the focus group also provided information supporting this finding. As it happens, each of the interviewees had responses that dealt with the subject of relevant issues and responses that dealt with making the church relevant. In one instance, Participant Five noted that the model addressed some things about which they desired to talk, but do not hear addressed in church, and in another Participant Six stated that the meetings provided a place to talk about life and not just church. Participant Two also commented on the attractive nature of the model by juxtaposing its result with young people who do not pay attention during the service thereby suggesting that young people do not pay attention to irrelevant ministry. In addition, Participant Seven recommended ways to ensure the relevance of ministry sessions by addressing personal challenges and world events. Each of the three data collection methods resulted in support for this finding that relevant content is important for relevant emerging adult ministry.

In addition, the model found that necessary for emerging adult ministry is the existence of a non-judgmental supportive community consisting of emerging adult peers with whom they have things in common. The study also found that successful emerging adult ministry also requires a non-judgmental, supportive community consisting of emerging adult members who have things in common. This community may utilize community building tools such as social media. To begin, the observations gathered during the model support this finding. The observations reported that social media is a contemporary method for reaching emerging adults, that the community was non-judgmental, and that the participants had much in common. In addition, the observations revealed that persons supported each other with encouragement when sharing their stories and that the sessions built a sense of community so much so that two persons who met during the model remain close.

Data derived from questionnaires provides support for this finding regarding community as well. After the model, 100% of participants agreed to having been in the midst of a supportive community by agreeing to the presence of people in their lives who will support and encourage them and with whom they could work out their beliefs. Also, 100% of respondents agreed to the importance of having people in their lives that will support them in their Christian journeys, and agreed that they could see the point in getting together with other young adult Christians—people with whom they had things in common. In addition, 75% of respondents agreed that they found a safe space where they could speak freely and not be judged while nearly every pre-test participant admitted to utilizing social media. Also, 87.5% of participants believed post-model that having persons of similar background and age to talk to helps them see the relevance of the church, while 75% believed that having a community of young adults makes the church feel more relevant. Overall, these data points reflect positive attitudinal change toward expected results.

The data supplied from interviews also supports this finding of the necessity of community. Every interview participant provided responses that fell into the category of supportive community with a majority also mentioning that the community was non-judgmental, was comprised of emerging adults with whom they shared commonalities, and social media. To this point, Participant Two enjoyed socializing with people her age and Participant Five highlighted the ability to talk with his peers about a situation. Also, Participant Seven talked about the ability in this setting to express herself without worrying about people looking at her while Participant One discussed never observing people condemning anybody during the sessions both of which reflected a non-judgmental community. On several occasions, respondents talked about members of the community reaching out to each other even outside of the sessions thereby demonstrating the spirit of a supportive community. In one of these instances the outreach took place utilizing social media, which the majority of those interviewed mentioned with regard to declaring relevant the methods for model advertisement. In total, the evidence supports the finding of the necessity of a non-judgmental, supportive community consisting of emerging adult peers who share commonalities.

Thirdly, the model found that ministry to emerging adults should include openness on the part of both leadership and participant where the integrity of such openness is protected by confidentiality. The data reveals a requirement for openness among ministry participants (emerging adult and leadership) in each tool as well as a need for confidentiality in two of three tools. Data from observations supports this finding. The model recorded that participants conversed openly about themselves and their desires. This included openly sharing their stories, discussing embarrassing details about themselves, opining on various topics, and vocalizing desires to leave their present contexts in a search for greater ministry. The observations also revealed concerns about confidentiality and the fact that openness on the part of leadership in some cases preceded openness on the part of participants. In addition to data from observations, data from questionnaires supports this finding. For example, 75% of participants agreed that in the context in question they found a safe space where they could speak freely, and 100% agreed that they had persons with whom they could work out their feeling suggesting a willingness to be open. At the same time, one participant expressed a desire for the church to address openness among members, while others described themselves as honest or straightforward thereby supporting the inclusion of openness in the list of ingredients for relevant emerging adult ministry.

Also, interviews served as a source of data that undergirds this finding of openness being necessary for relevant emerging adult ministry. Nearly all of those interviewed, expressed some sentiment that fell into the category of addressing openness among the model participants while all of them in some form or another alluded to the openness of leadership. Only one of those persons interviewed mentioned confidentiality noting its importance. Participant Four noted that he did not feel like he needed to be uptight, but could open up after others did the same, and Participant Seven credited the supportive community as the reason why she opened up while blaming an unwillingness to open up for the premature exit of a few persons. Others credited transparent and open leadership as helping them to be more open and stated that such openness on the part of leadership made the experience feel more relevant. When combined, the evidence provided from the three methods of data collection give credence to the inclusion of openness as a requirement for relevant emerging adult ministry.

The fourth major finding is that ministry to emerging adults should have a design similar to the model of ministry. This conclusion finds evidence in all three forms of data collection, and finds support in data that discusses emerging adult attraction and retention in or as a result of the model and persons' desire to continue individual sessions and the model of ministry beyond the initially scheduled timeframe. Observations support this finding in that twenty-one emerging adults provided data—seventeen of whom the model successfully attracted to attend at least one session with most of these coming after the initial session. The fact that eight participants attended three sessions or more demonstrated the model's success in retaining some of those who began to participate. At the same time, the observed behavior of the emerging adults in the sessions who pushed for more discussion instead of leaving early several times and who stayed at the context for three hours demonstrating a desire to continue the sessions. The model observed participants stating openly and to each other on several occasions that the model should continue or keep going beyond the six weeks.

When it came to questionnaires, participants at the final session also unanimously agreed that the model should continue past the original limited schedule of six weeks. Questionnaires also support this finding as 75% of focus group participants grew to agree that they found a safe space in the church where they could speak freely and not be judged or a welcoming place. This was in spite of their feeling that older people in the church would keep them or have kept them from being involved in the church. Furthermore, the questionnaires and interviews led to the discovery of the fact that Participant Two considered leaving the church of interest until her participation in this model; therefore the model led to her retention at the church. In addition, Participant Five reported that texting was the most effective means of attracting persons to the sessions suggesting that other methods were also effective. On the other hand, persons repeatedly stated in interviews that the sessions would have been better with more people suggesting that that the model could have been more effective in advertising or attracting emerging adults. Furthermore, Participant Two noted that they were able to stay as long as they desired indicating that they only stayed because they desired for the sessions to continue. Also, interviewed participants unanimously agreed that the model should continue beyond the six weeks. Now that this chapter has revealed a recipe for the problem at the center of this book, the next chapter reflects over the research, summarizes the impacts, and looks forward to the possibilities for emerging adult ministry.

NOTES

[1] John W. Creswell, *Research Design: Qualitative, Quantitative, and Mixed Method Approaches*, 3rd (Thousand Oaks, CA: SAGE Publications, 2009), 13.
[2] Ibid., 177.
[3] Ibid.
[4] Ibid., 178.
[5] Ibid., 181.
[6] Ibid., 179.
[7] Ibid., 181-182.
[8] Ibid., 183.
[9] Ibid.
[10] Ibid., 184.
[11] Ibid.
[12] Ibid.
[13] Ibid.
[14] Ibid., 185-190.
[15] Ibid., 185.
[16] Ibid.
[17] Ibid., 186.
[18] Ibid.
[19] Ibid., 189.
[20] Ibid.
[21] Ibid.
[22] Ibid.
[23] Ibid.
[24] Ibid.
[25] Ibid., 191.

CHAPTER SEVEN
LOOKING BACK AND LOOKING FORWARD

The previous chapter revealed a recipe for young adult attraction and retention that included relevant content, community, openness, and a design similar to the model of ministry. Based on the aforementioned definition of success, this study was successful because at the conclusion of this study, the analysis of the data led to the discovery of the necessary ingredients for emerging adult attraction and retention. These ingredients, as listed in the major findings in the section above, include relevant content, community, and openness. When combined with the fourth and final major finding, clearly churches desiring to attract and retain emerging adults would find this model helpful. This is because an examination of the data leads to a refined hypothesis that states having a ministry for emerging adults that has the ingredients of relevant content, community, and openness will lead to the attraction and retention of emerging adults in churches.

To review, the model of ministry contained two sermons both of which highlighted the need for relevant ministry and argued in support of the model of ministry using Old Testament and New Testament biblical foundations. The model of ministry also involved six sessions where emerging adults met weekly to discuss relevant issues, enjoy each other's' company by conversing and playing games, and be open and transparent with each other. To be clear, the model included such sessions for the purpose of making the church relevant and facilitating the construction of community among the participants. The model used flyers and technology (text messaging and social media) to advertise events and communicate with potential and actual participants.

This ministry led to the evolution of my theology, and led to my learning important lessons about emerging adults and this ministry. This model transformed me in giving me an opportunity to address something that has bothered me for a very long time. It has also transformed my view of the church by thoroughly convincing me that God's design for ministry includes relevance, community and transparency. These elements for the church are rooted in her history and to remain relevant the church should continue to hold them dear. This model has taught me that in the presence of such community people can feel free to express themselves, support each other and have their holistic concerns addressed. Furthermore, this model reinforces the belief that the church must partner with God and with each other in order to get what she needs especially by engaging in community and focusing on relevant content. This model clearly communicated that relevance will lead emerging adults to pay attention and give them the desire to remain on contact with such ministry. The ingredients listed above are not just helpful for emerging adult ministry, but for all ministry as evidenced by copycatting by the ministries for men and women. If the church is to survive, she must embrace the call to include these elements lest not simply emerging adults fall away, but the other adult demographics as well. While this Christian journey is an individual journey, God has not designed Christians to walk this journey alone.

In addition, this model taught me through research into theoretical sources as well as through experience that emerging adults are a non-monolithic group. At the same time, emerging adults are not monolithic when it comes to how to communicate with them technologically speaking where some responded better to phone calls, text messaging, or social media. Put another way, emerging adults have a great deal of diversity, but it is my belief that they all want relevant content, community and openness in their interactions in church. Based on the data analysis, emerging adults also want to be made to feel important and empowered to have a hand in choosing their activities and this goes back to the theme of partnership. Partnering with leadership seemed to make the ministry feel more relevant to them. The model also taught me about the important role of leadership when ministering to emerging adults. Leadership must be willing to participate in activities including offering honest opinions on topics, sharing in community, and engaging in transparency especially about past failures and doubts. At one point the emerging adult participants were asked why they had not been in contact in order to ask for more sessions after unanimously agreeing that the ministry should continue. After responding with a request for another session, they taught me that leadership must push such ministry and get events on their calendars in order for it to continue. Perhaps this suggests that emerging adults are very busy and do not seek more things in which to participate, but they must be invited to participate. Also, the model taught me that prior relationships matter when it comes to building trust. Some people will reject invitations to participate as they did with Hezekiah, but rejection should not prevent effort.

When considering what the model taught me in conjunction with the previous design, some changes would be in order to improve the model. For instance, the model should be longer by two weeks. In addition to the events already included, the model should include another community building activity other than the game nights or "Sharing Our Stories" session. The model should also have another session focused on personal issues experienced by participants along with world events. Perhaps, as suggested by one of my professional associates Faith Harris, womanist methodology could be used to analyze the stories of emerging adults who participate in order to "derive theo-ethical principles for teaching and praxis." After the conclusion of the model, the next ministry session that was held focused on things in the news and seemed to go over well. The model should also end with another sermon that deals with a specific topic relevant to emerging adults. The order of events would therefore include, a sermon, four weeks of activities, a second sermon, an additional four weeks of activities, and a final sermon respectively. If given another opportunity, the model would encourage more social media engagement to reinforce the feeling of community perhaps by establishing a group page on Facebook. Along the same lines, the model would establish a text messaging account to be able to communicate words of encouragement, share prayer requests, and reports of success. Transparency on the part of leadership would increase to be more open about past failures and current doubts. The model would utilize additional advertising methods after securing more funding in the budget for this purpose.

Persons interested in conducting future research in this vein should utilize and test the final hypothesis and conduct a yearlong mixed-method study with this ministry meeting on a regular basis. The correlation between ministry participation and Sunday worship attendance should be tracked along with gains and losses in emerging adult membership. All emerging adult participants should sit for entrance and exit interviews that would respectively focus on their reasons for entering and remaining with or departing from the ministry. These reasons should be compared and contrasted with the ingredients presented in the final hypothesis in order to compile list of ingredients that kept them or attracted them as well as the ingredients that led to their departure. Such research would provide a clearer picture of what churches need in order to attract and retain emerging adults.

The results of such a study could have a lasting impact on society and the church in her efforts to restore her missing population. In the words of Penny Edgell, "There is no debate among social scientists about the generally positive effects that religious involvement has on a range of life-outcomes: reduced crime, delinquency, and depression; increased well-being; increased happiness and satisfaction in one's life and with one's marriage and family relationships; marital stability; civic involvement; and general health."[1] Not only would the end goal of this research benefit society at large, but also it stands to benefit the local church and the church as a whole. As noted previously, McIntosh was correct in essentially stating that emerging adults of today will lead our churches tomorrow.[2] A failure on the part of the church to attract and retain emerging adults will lead to a vacuum of leadership and stagnation within the church. Stephens and Watkins rightly wrote that young adults "are the church's future, and the church that fails to develop its young adults is a church that will not have a future. Therefore active care for and involvement of young adults must begin now."[3] However, this is true not only for African American churches as they wrote, but for all churches.

On the other hand, if the church utilizes the research contained within this presentation as a model for attracting and retaining emerging adults the church can usher in new people with fresh ideas and different perspectives that are critical for leadership of the church in this age. Growing this particular demographic provides a ministry to which teenagers and even pre-teens can aspire to be a part. At the same time, keeping emerging adults active in the church, including by occupying leadership positions, would provide a pipeline to other positions of leadership as well as more productive and active adults. A strong emerging adult ministry should perhaps mean that every demographic has relevant ministry both at the global and local church levels. Without this critical demographic, the church is incomplete and therefore it cannot have the maximum amount of impact in the world being at less than full strength. This church could also use this recipe to produce effective ministry to any demographic in the church. This research resulted in a portable and repeatable model of ministry that crosses denominations and ethnic boundaries within the church because the appearance of these ingredients can look differently in different contexts. For example, what is relevant to a twenty-five year old African American man on the South Side of Chicago may differ from what is relevant to a nineteen year old Caucasian woman in rural Kansas.

The possible impacts on individual emerging adults cannot be overstated where such ministry should provide relevant content and the community setting that would provide support, encouragement, and a safe space to wrestle with all that affects them during this critical period in their lives. Ministry for emerging adults must possess the necessary appeal and relevance to attract and retain emerging adults with the understanding that simply attracting or solely retaining will still fail to sufficiently stock churches with emerging adults all of whom could make a difference. The stated purpose of the study was to explore the ingredients necessary for attraction and retention of emerging adults in a model of ministry in order to arrive at a hypothesis for what is necessary to produce this in the larger church. The aim of this work was not to be the final solution for this persistent problem, but one of its goals was to offer a contribution to the conversation and debate while giving voice to voiceless emerging adults. In that regard, among others, this work succeeds.

NOTES

[1] Penny Edgell, "Faith and Spirituality among Emerging Adults," accessed September 3, 2014, http://doc.wrlc.org/bitstream/handle/2041/122309/Edgell_Faith.pdf?sequence=1.

[2] Gary L. McIntosh, *One Church, Four Generations: Understanding and Reaching All Ages in Your Church* (Grand Rapids, MI: Baker Books, 2002), 137.

[3] Benjamin Stephens III and Ralph C. Watkins, *From Jay-Z to Jesus: Reaching and Teaching Young Adults in the Black Church* (Valley Forge, PA: Judson Press, 2009), 9.

APPENDIX A
PROJECT FORMS

APPENDIX A

Emerging Adult Attraction & Retention
Information Sheet

Purpose: The study is concerned with exploring ways to make the church and Christianity more relevant to young adults between the ages of eighteen and thirty. The belief is that by increasing the relevance of the church and the Christian faith to young adults, it will lead to more young adults being attracted and retained by the church.

Vital facts of the study:

- The study will involve six weeks of activities and two sermons. Each session will last for approximately two hours. Data will be collected in the form of surveys, interviews, and observations. The researcher's mentors and faculty consultant have reviewed and given their approval for this study.

- You have been asked to participate because you are between the ages of eighteen and thirty and can provide feedback as to whether or not the study increases the sense of relevance of the church and Christianity to persons in your age group.

- Your participation is voluntary. However, your participation is greatly appreciated as your candid responses will lead to a more relevant ministry in churches. By signing the consent form you would be agreeing to allow the researcher to use your feedback for analysis and inclusion in the researcher's doctoral project. In particular, if asked and accepting of the invitation to participate in an in-depth interview, your responses may be quoted and or included in the final project verbatim. If you become uncomfortable with any of your responses you are free to contact the researcher to have some or all of your interview feedback removed. You will receive a copy of both this sheet and the consent form for your records.

- Your responses will be cloaked in anonymity. No one will be able to deduce from your responses your exact identity. If the researcher chooses to use quotes from your feedback, their inclusion in the final project will be anonymous. The data or feedback that you provide will be kept confidential and shielded from public view for the duration of the study. Only the researcher will have access to all of the raw data. After the project is completed, your responses will be retained for the researcher's records for up to six months.

- The results will be included in the final D.Min. project. They will be reviewed by the examination committee. Future students in the same program may read this research. The final project will also likely be published in various forms.

- I do not foresee any disadvantages of taking part in this study. At the conclusion of the study, you may be asked to sit for an interview to provide more in-depth responses with regard to your experience. If there are any concerns, please contact the researcher whose contact information is provided below.

For Further Information Contact:
Nicholas Meade • Cell: [REDACTED] • Email: [REDACTED] • FB: [REDACTED] • Twitter: [REDACTED]

If you agree to take part in the study, please sign the consent form on the other side.

APPENDIX A

Consent Form

I, _____ (print), agree to participate in Nicholas Meade's research study.

I understand and have record of the essential facts of this study.

I am between the ages of eighteen and thirty (Age: _____)

I offer my participation voluntarily

I will provide feedback that will remain anonymous

I agree to the condition that only the researcher will have access to all of the raw data and to his retention of this data for up to six months in a protected form

I agree to be interviewed at my convenience if I give permission:
    (Please check only one box:)
    I agree to be interviewed at my convenience
    I do not agree to be interviewed at my convenience

If agreeable to an interview and I am interviewed, I understand that feedback provided through my interview may be used and included anonymously in Nicholas Meade's final project and or published form if I give permission:

    (Please check only one box:)
    ☐ I agree to the inclusion of data provided during my interview

    ☐ I do not agree to the inclusion of data provided during my interview

I agree to contact Nicholas Meade if I require more information or wish to have my input withdrawn from the study

Signed _____
Date _____

APPENDIX A

Getting To Know You...

Name: _____

You will be asked to stand and share your answers with the group. After this, we will break into pairs and you will get to mingle, talk about your answers and discuss what you have in common with the other person. Answer this follow-up question with your partner: what do we have in common?

1. What is your first name and last initial?

2. What is your nickname (if you have one)?

3. What about your family? (siblings, children, spouse, etc.)

4. What social media sites have you joined?

5. What are you doing with your life now? (work, school, etc.) Where?

6. Where do you want to be 10 years from now?

7. What are the three words that best describe you?

8. What are some issues that you'd like to see addressed in churches?

9. What is your passion?

10. Favorite musical artist? Sport? Food?

11. What do you do for fun?

12. What is one thing (embarrassing or not) that not everyone knows about you?

APPENDIX B
EMERGING ADULT MODEL MINISTRY SURVEY

APPENDIX B

EMERGING ADULT MODEL MINISTRY SURVEY

Please take some time to complete this survey. Your identity will be kept confidential. We appreciate your participation. We hope this will lead to better ministry options for churches. In this survey, emerging adults are young adults 18-30. The word "relevant" means that it connects with who you are and what matters to you. Community refers to togetherness and helping each other. Holistic refers to things that concern the whole person. Spiritual refers to one's relationship with God.

Thank you!

Name: _____

Is [REDACTED] the church to which you belong? Y   N

Age: _____

Gender: M   F

Statement	Strongly Agree	Agree	Neutral / Not Sure	Disagree	Strongly Disagree
I feel that church is relevant for my life					
I can see the relevance of the Christian faith to my life as an young adult					

I believe that having a community of young adults makes the church feel more relevant						
I sense that having persons of similar background and age to talk to helps me see the relevance of church						
I feel the church should address holistic issues						
I desire to leave the church as soon as I am given the choice to do so.						
I desire to leave my church to attend another as soon as I am given the choice to do so						

APPENDIX B

I believe that community is absent from the church					
I think that older people in the church will keep me or have kept me from being more involved in the church					
I think that the church addresses various concerns of my life and not just the spiritual					
I sense that people need others to help them be better Christians					
I feel like changes to worship services need to be introduced for me to feel as if the church is relevant					

I feel that God cares about my whole life and not just the spiritual part of me					
I feel like the Bible has relevance to my life					
I believe that I need people around me who will encourage me to do the right thing and please God					
I believe this emerging adult period of my life is important to the rest of my life					
I have friends who do not attend church because they do not find it relevant					

Additional Comments:

APPENDIX C
INTERVIEW QUESTIONS

APPENDIX C

Interview Questions

Name: _____

1. How do feel about the project that has taken place over the course of the last six weeks?

Do you believe that these six weeks have helped you see the relevance of the church? How so? Is relevance important for attracting and retaining young adults? Do you believe that during the past six weeks you've discussed relevant issues and this made the church feel more relevant? Why or why not? Do you believe that the activities of the last six weeks have helped you? Why or why not? What was the best part of the last six weeks of activities? Why or why not?

2. How would you describe the sense of community?

Did you feel like you found a community that had a safe space with people whom you could be honest and share your stories? Why or why not? Do you believe that being in community with these persons makes it more likely for you to remain active in the church? Why or why not? Do you believe you've met people that can help you reach your dreams and become a better Christian or be more like Jesus? Why or why not? Did you believe that the community was supportive or that it was judgmental? Why or why not? Have you met people with whom you desire to remain connected? Why or why not? Do you believe that sharing your stories made you feel more connected to the other participants? Why or why not?

3. What feedback would you provide about the job the leader did?

Do you believe the leader was transparent and willing to take on controversial subjects? If so, do you believe that transparent leadership and the leader's willingness to be open and honest while tackling controversial subjects and the holistic concerns of young adults made this experience feel more relevant? Why or why not?

4. What impact has this project had on you? What impact do you foresee on young adults if this type of thing continued here or was implemented elsewhere?

APPENDIX C

As the result of this model do you believe that you have a greater chance to remain faithful to being a Christian? Why or why not? How would you describe your experience in this project? Could you see yourself being drawn to this church or another church with a similar ministry? Or if you belong to this church, does having a ministry like this increase the odds that you will stay around? Why or why not?

5. Should this ministry continue? Why or why not? If so, would you want to continue attending? In what ways could the last six weeks have been better? What would you do to improve this going forward? Why or why not? Do you believe that the methods used to advertise these events were relevant? Why or why not?

APPENDIX D
YOUNG ADULT ACTIVITIES FLYER

APPENDIX D

Special Young Adult Activities

For Young Adults Ages 18—30

Come and meet with other young adults between the ages of 18 and 30! Get to know some people for the purpose of knowing other Christian young adults who know what you're going through and can be there for you!

All events to be held at 5pm.
Food or refreshments will be served at each event.

2/15—Young Adult Meet, Greet & Game Night
2/22—Why the Bible and Church is Relevant
3/1—Sharing Our Stories—discussing victories of the past, present & future
3/8—Rap Session—discussing holistic concerns of young adults
3/15—Game night
3/22—Reflection and wrap-up

de·**bate**
con·ver·sa·tion

For more information, contact:
Rev. Nicholas A. Meade • Cell: • FB: • Twitter:

APPENDIX E
DATA COLLECTION CHARTS AND GRAPHS

APPENDIX E

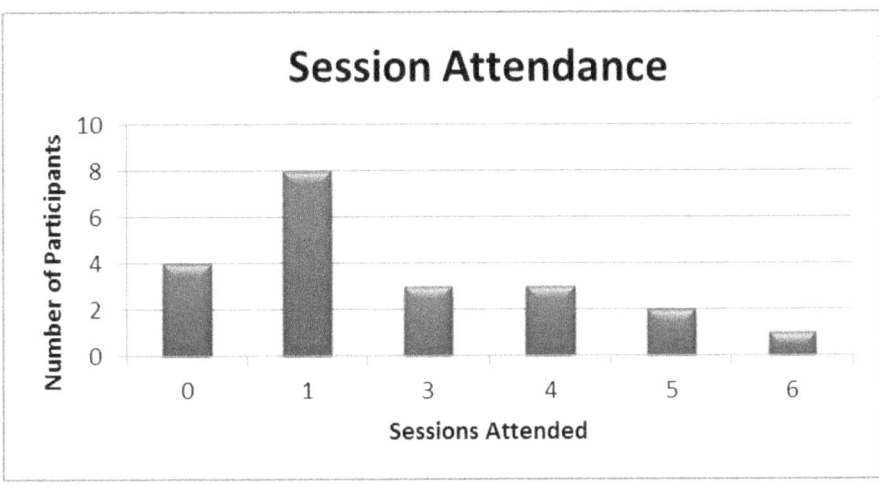

Figure 1

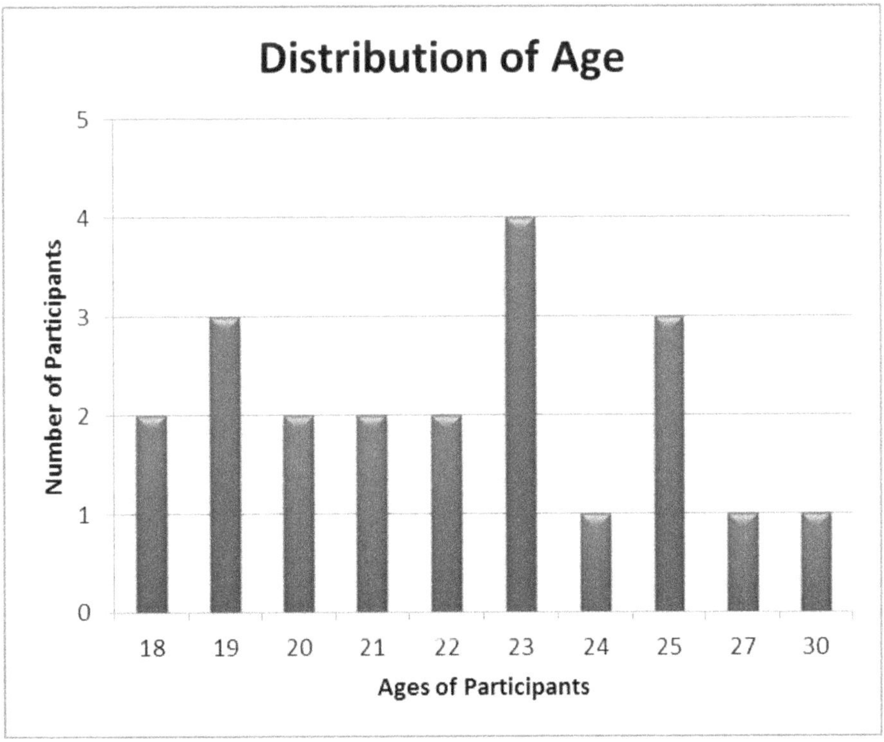

Figure 2

APPENDIX E

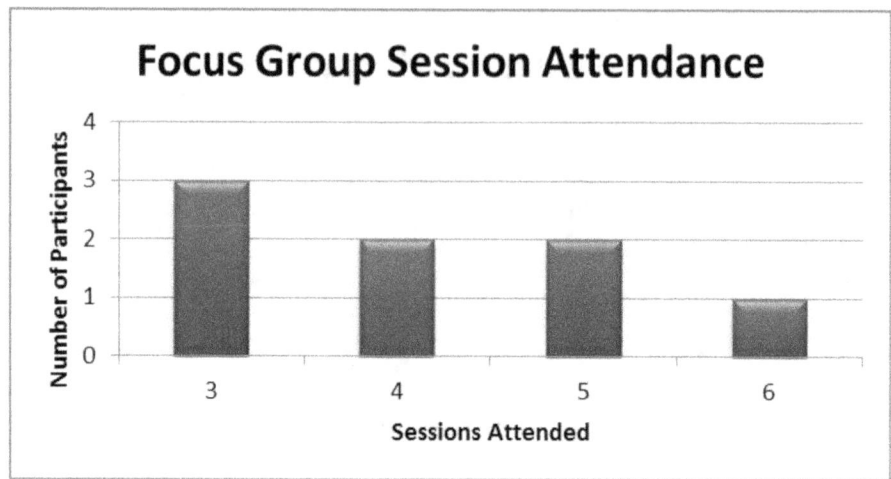

Figure 3

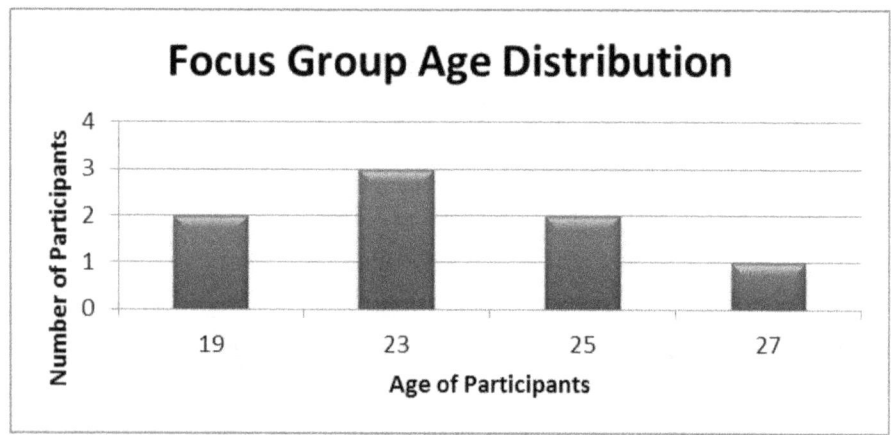

Figure 4

APPENDIX E

Table 1 – Test Statements

Statement #	Statement
Statement 1	I feel that church is relevant for my life
Statement 2	I have people in my life who will support and encourage me and with whom I can work out my feelings and beliefs
Statement 3	I can see the relevance of the Christian faith to my life as an young adult
Statement 4	I believe that having a community of young adults makes the church feel more relevant
Statement 5	I sense that having persons of similar background and age to talk to helps me see the relevance of church
Statement 6	I feel that having people in my life who will support me in my Christian journey is important
Statement 7	I feel that churches aren't capable of making the church and the Bible relevant to young adults
Statement 8	I can see the point of getting together with other young adult Christians
Statement 9	I believe that community is absent from my church
Statement 10	I feel lonely, isolated or alone in my journey
Statement 11	I think that the church addresses all of my concerns
Statement 12	I believe that I have not encountered anyone or any ministry that deals with what's important to me
Statement 13	I sense that I am connected with people that I know can help me in my journey as a Christian
Statement 14	I feel that God cares about my whole life and not just the spiritual part of me
Statement 15	I feel like the Bible has principles and stories that are applicable to my life
Statement 16	I believe that I need people around me who will encourage me to do the right thing and please God
Statement 17	I think that I do not need anyone's help in my journey
Statement 18	I feel like in this church I've found a safe space (not necessarily the whole church) where I can speak freely and not be judged

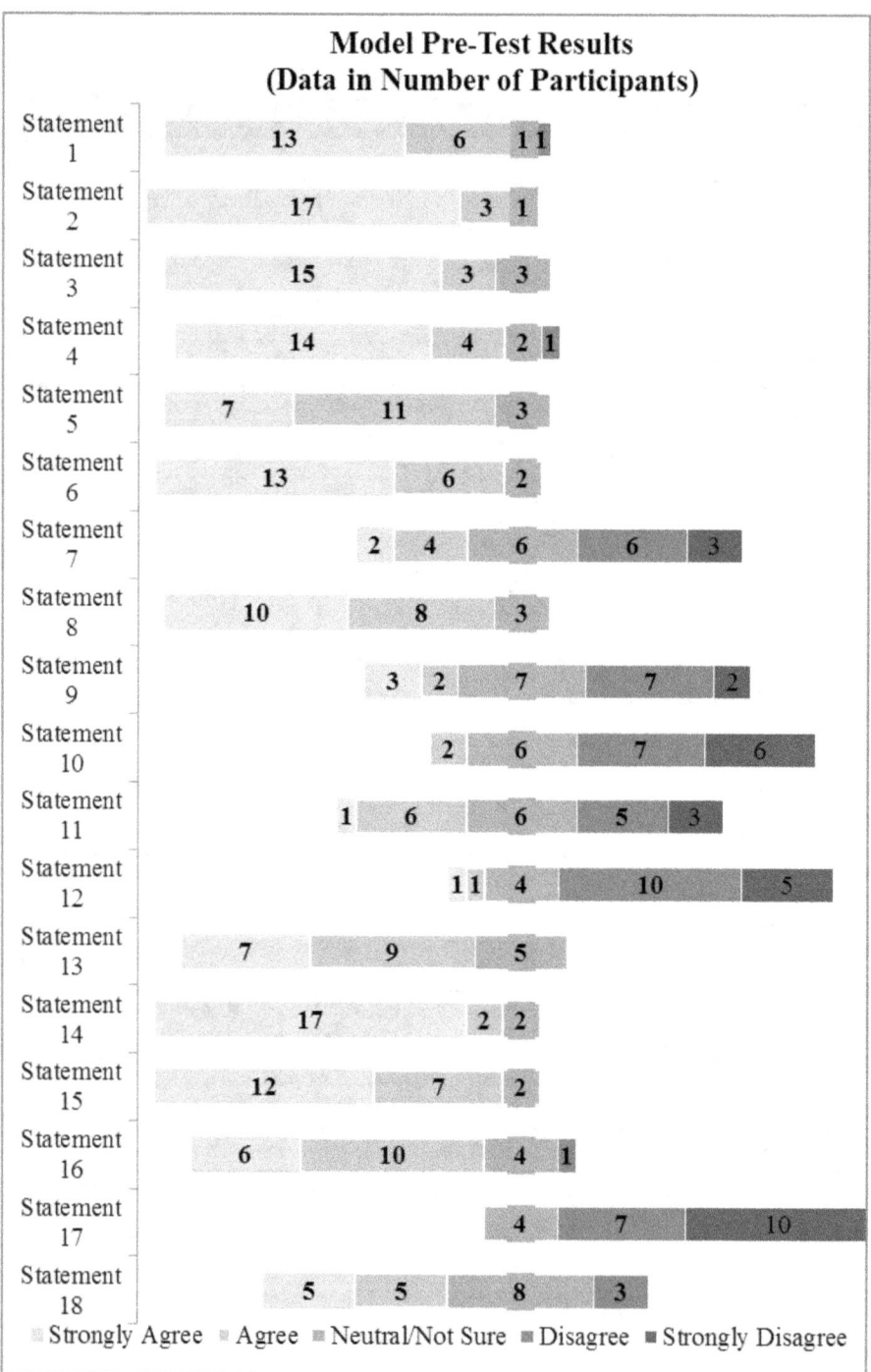

Figure 5

APPENDIX E

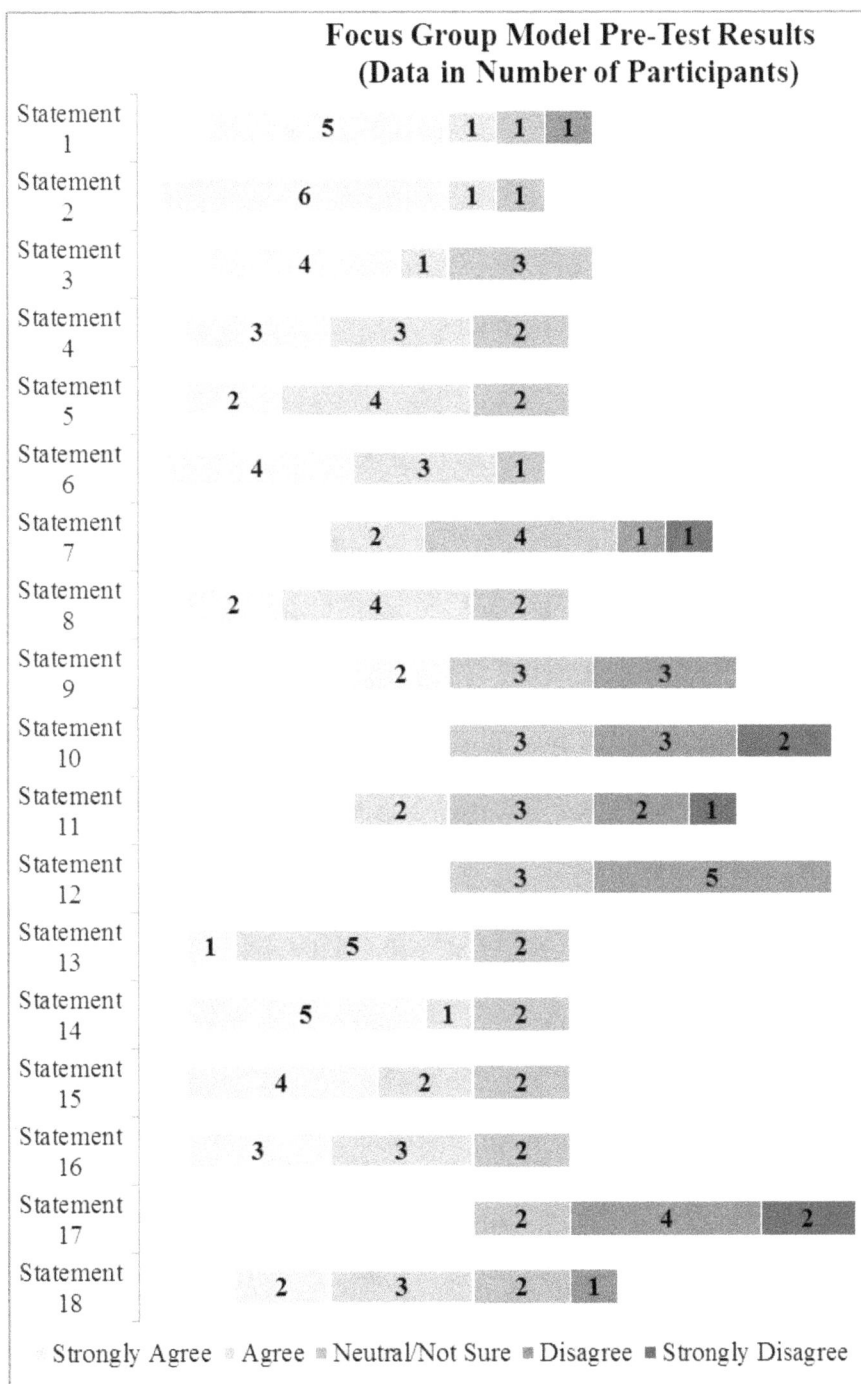

Figure 6

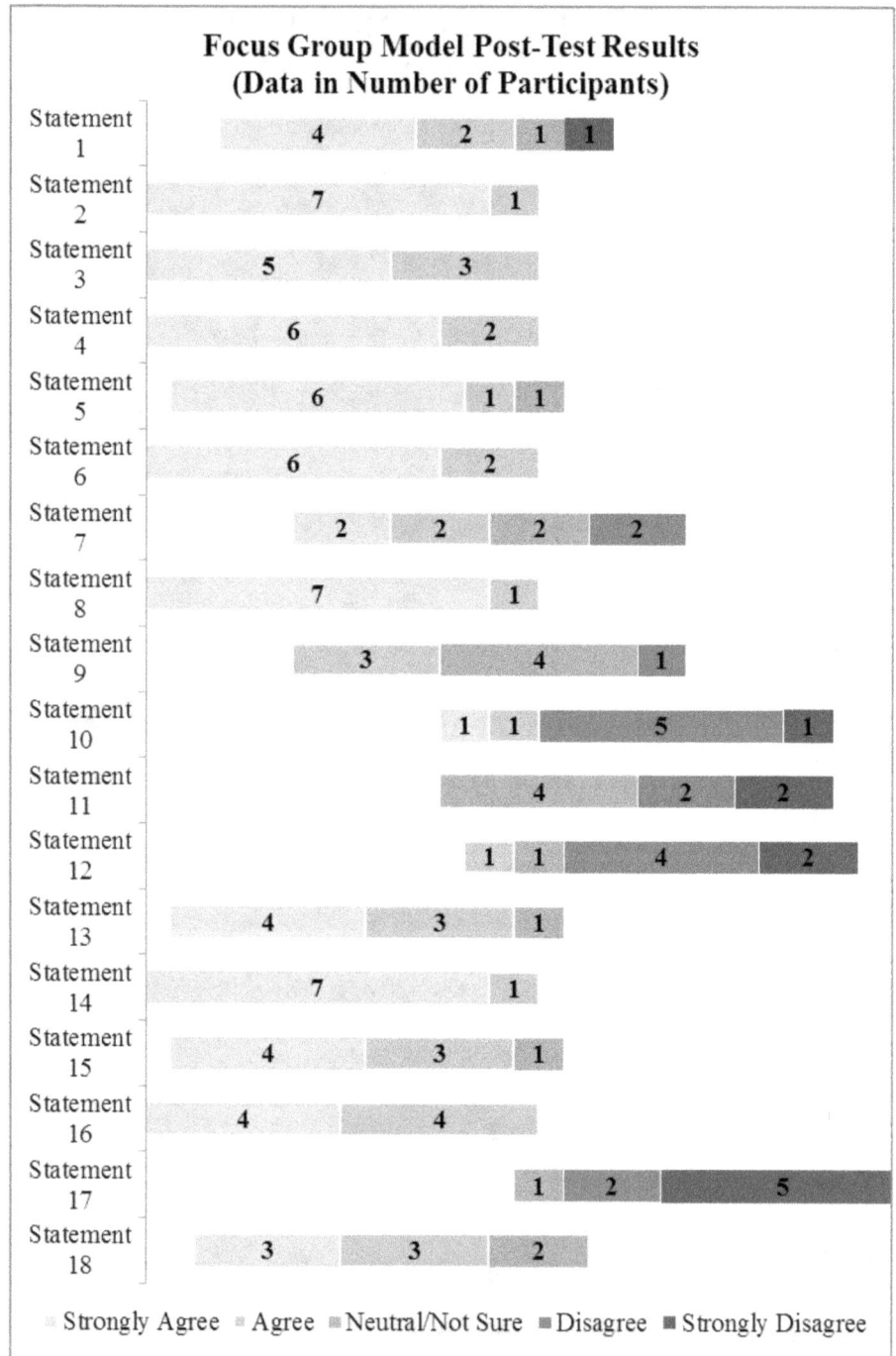

Figure 7

APPENDIX E

Table 2 – Focus Group Profiles

Alias	Age	Gender	Marital Status	Has Children	Context Associate	Sessions Attended
Participant 1	23	Male	Single	No	Yes	6
Participant 2	25	Female	Single	Yes	No	4
Participant 3	19	Female	Single	No	Yes	3
Participant 4	19	Male	Single	No	No	3
Participant 5	23	Male	Single	Yes	No	4
Participant 6	25	Male	Married	Yes	No	5
Participant 7	27	Female	Married	Yes	No	5
Participant 8	23	Female	Single	No	No	3

Table 3 – Profile Sheet Feedback

Issues Participants Desired for Churches to Address
How to handle doubt
The importance of living good
Understanding the Bible
Gossiping
Cliques
Balancing life and church
Gay rights and church rights
Openness
Mental health
Provocative dress
Finances
Afterhours activities
Controversial topics
Parenting
Churches leave young adults feeling left out or as if their very presence is irrelevant
How churches place youth and young adults together as they are at the context of interest when they do not face the same problems
Methods for getting youth (likely meant young adults) involved
Judgmental or condemning attitudes (2)
Issues relevant for young adults or real world problems (2)
Fake people or hypocrisy (3)
Relationships (4)

BIBLIOGRAPHY

Ackermann, Denise. "Liberation and Practical Theology: A Feminist Perspective on Ministry." *Journal Of Theology For Southern Africa* no. 52 (September 1, 1985): 30-41. *ATLA Religion Database with ATLASerials*, EBSCO*host*. Accessed September 15, 2013.

Alsup, John E. "Prayer, Consciousness, and the Early Church: A Look at Acts 2:41-47 for today." *Austin Seminary Bulletin (Faculty Ed.)* 101, no. 4 (October 1, 1985): 31-37. *ATLA Religion Database with ATLASerials*, EBSCO*host*. Accessed March 4, 2013.

Anderson, Justice C. "Church and Liberation Theology." *Southwestern Journal Of Theology* 19, no. 2 (March 1, 1977): 17-36. *ATLA Religion Database with ATLASerials*, EBSCO*host*. Accessed September 15, 2013.

Arnett, Jeffrey Jensen. *Adolescence and Emerging Adulthood: A Cultural Approach*. 3rd. Upper Saddle River, NJ: Pearson, 2007.

Aronen, Jaakko. "Indebtedness to Passio Perpetuae in Pontius' Vita Cypriani." *Vigiliae Christianae* 38, no. 1 (March 1, 1984): 67-76. *ATLA Religion Database with ATLASerials*, EBSCO*host*. Accessed March 6, 2013.

Augustine and Walter Shewring. *The Passion of SS. Perpetua and Felicity, MM: A New Edition and Translation of the Latin Text, Together with the Sermons of St. Augustine Upon These Saints, Now First Translated into English*. London, UK: Sheed and Ward, 1931.

Baker, David L. "The Jubilee and the Millennium." *Themelios,* October 1998.

Barry, Carolyn McNamara, and Stephanie D. Madsen. "Friends and Friendships in Emerging Adulthood." 2010. Accessed at September 4, 2014, http://doc.wrlc.org/bitstream/handle/2041/122313/Barry-Madsen_Friends.pdf?sequence=1.

Bartchy, S. Scott. "Divine Power, Community Formation, and Leadership in Acts" In *Community Formation in the Early Church and in the Church Today*. Edited by Richard N. Longenecker. Peabody, MA: Hendrickson, 2002.

Baugh, Ken and Rich Hurst. *Getting Real: An Interactive Guide to Relational Ministry*. Colorado Springs, CO: NavPress, 2000.

Beaty, Katelyn, and Christian Smith. "Lost in Transition: With His Latest Research on Emerging Adults, Sociologist Christian Smith Helps The Church Reach Out to a Rootless Generation." *Christianity Today* 53, no. 10 (October 1, 2009): 34-37. *ATLA Religion Database with ATLASerials*, EBSCO*host*. Accessed September 25, 2013.

Beaudoin, Tom. *Virtual Faith: The Irreverent Spiritual Quest of Generation X*. San Francisco, CA: Jossey-Bass, 1998.

Bedford, Nancy Elizabeth. "Fidelidad y deslealtad: testimonio martirial y pastoral profética." *Cuadernos De Teología* 24, (January 1, 2005): 139-152. *ATLA Religion Database with ATLASerials*, EBSCO*host*. Accessed March 6, 2013.

Benner, David G., and Peter C. Hill, eds. *Baker Encyclopedia of Psychology & Counseling*. Grand Rapids, MI: Baker Books, 1999.

Bergant, Dianne. *People of the Covenant: An Invitation to the Old Testament*. Franklin, WI: Sheed & Ward, 2001.

Boff, Leonardo, and Paul Burns. "Trinitarian Community and Social Liberation." *Cross Currents* 38, no. 3 (September 1, 1988): 289-308. *ATLA Religion Database with ATLASerials*, EBSCO*host*. Accessed September 15, 2013.

Boff, Leonardo. *Jesus Christ Liberator: A Critical Christology for Our Time*. Translated by Patrick Hughes. Maryknoll, NY: Orbis Books, 1978.

_____. *Faith on the Edge: Religion and Marginalized Existence*. Translated by Robert R. Barr. Maryknoll, NY: Orbis Books, 1991.

Bowers, Laurene Beth. *Designing Contemporary Congregations: Strategies to Attract Those under Fifty*. Cleveland, OH: Pilgrim Press, 2008.

Bradshaw, Paul F. "The Gospel and the Catechumenate in the Third Century." *Journal Of Theological Studies* 50, no. 1 (April 1, 1999): 143-152. *ATLA Religion Database with ATLASerials*, EBSCO*host*. Accessed March 6, 2013.

Brooks, David. "The Odyssey Years." *New York Times*, October 9, 2007. Accessed October 28, 2013. http://www.nytimes.com/2007/10/09/opinion/09brooks.html?_r=0.

Butler, Rex D. The New Prophecy & "New Visions". Vol. 18 of North American Patristic Society Patristic Monograph Series, edited by Philip Rousseau. Washington, DC: The Catholic University of America Press, 2006.

Byrd, Nathan C, III. "Narrative Discipleship: Guiding Emerging Adults to 'Connect the dots' of life and faith." *Christian Education Journal* 8, no. 2 (September 1, 2011): 244-262. *ATLA Religion Database with ATLASerials*, EBSCO*host*. Accessed September 25, 2013.

BIBLIOGRAPHY

Cardman, Francine. "Acts of the women martyrs." *Anglican Theological Review* 70, no. 2 (April 1, 1988): 144-150. *ATLA Religion Database with ATLASerials*, EBSCO*host*. Accessed March 6, 2013.

Carroll, Colleen. *The New Faithful: Why Young Adults are Embracing Christian Orthodoxy*. Chicago, IL: Loyola Press, 2002.

Chapman, G Clarke, Jr. "Bonhoeffer : Resource for Liberation Theology." *Union Seminary Quarterly Review* 36, no. 4 (June 1, 1981): 225-242. *ATLA Religion Database with ATLASerials*, EBSCO*host*. Accessed September 15, 2013.

Chavel, Simeon. "The Second Passover, Pilgrimage, and the Centralized Cult." *Harvard Theological Review* 102, no. 1 (January 1, 2009): 1-24. *ATLA Religion Database with ATLASerials*, EBSCO*host*. Accessed September 3, 2014.

Coggins, R. J. *The First and Second Books of the Chronicles*. New York, NY: Cambridge University Press, 1976.

Conn, Harvie M. "Theologies of Liberation: Towards a Common View," in *Tensions in Contemporary Theology*. 2nd ed., Edited by Stanley N. Gundry and Alan F. Johnson. Grand Rapids, MI: Baker Book House, 1976.

Coogan, Michael D. *The New Oxford Annotated Bible*. New York, NY: Oxford University Press, 2007.

Creswell, John W. *Research Design: Qualitative, Quantitative, and Mixed Method Approaches.* 3rd. Thousand Oaks, CA: SAGE Publications, 2009.

Cross, F. L., and Elizabeth A. Livingstone. *The Oxford Dictionary of the Christian Church*. New York, NY: Oxford University Press, 2005.

De Vries, Simon J. *1 and 2 Chronicles*. Vol. XI, *The Forms of the Old Testament Literature*, Grand Rapids, MI: Wm. B. Eerdmans Publishing Co., 1989.

Dierberg, Jill, and Lynn Schofield Clark. "Media in the Lives of Young Adults: Implications for Religious Organizations." Accessed at October 28, 2013. http://www.changingsea.net/essays/Dierberg.pdf.

Dillard, Raymond B. *2 Chronicles*. Vol. 15, *World Biblical Commentary*, Waco, TX: Word Books, 1987.

Dillon, Richard J. "Acts of the Apostles" In *The New Jerome Biblical Commentary*, edited by Raymond E. Brown, Joseph A. Fitzmyer, and Roland E. Murphy. Old Tappan, NJ: Pearson, 1990, 724-725.

Dronke, Peter. *Women Writers of the Middle Ages.* Cambridge, UK: Cambridge University Press, 1984.

Eagleson, John. "Orbis Books and Liberation Theology." *American Theological Library Association Summary Of Proceedings* 39, (January 1, 1985): 130-140. *ATLA Religion Database with ATLASerials*, EBSCO*host*. Accessed September 15, 2013.

Edgell, Penny. "Faith and Spirituality among Emerging Adults." 2009. Accessed September 3, 2014. http://doc.wrlc.org/bitstream/handle/2041/122309/Edgell_Faith.pdf?sequence=1.

Elwell, Walter A., and Barry J. Beitzel, *Baker Encyclopedia of the Bible*. Grand Rapids, MI: Baker Book House, 1988.

Escobar, Samuel. "Beyond Liberation Theology: Evangelical Missiology in Latin America." *International Bulletin Of Missionary Research* 6, no. 3 (July 1, 1982): 108-114. *ATLA Religion Database with ATLASerials*, EBSCO*host*. Accessed September 15, 2013.

Feldman, Louis H. "Josephus's Portrait of Hezekiah." *Journal Of Biblical Literature* 111, no. 4 (December 1, 1992): 597-610. *ATLA Religion Database with ATLASerials*, EBSCO*host*. Accessed May 19, 2013.

Ferguson, Sinclair B., and J.I. Packer. *New Dictionary of Theology*. Downers Grove, IL: InterVarsity Press, 2000.

Finger, Reta Halteman. "A Theology of Welcome: The Hospitable Hidden Women of Acts 2, 4, and 6." *Conrad Grebel Review* 23, no. 1 (December 1, 2005): 30-41. *ATLA Religion Database with ATLASerials*, EBSCO*host*. Accessed February 13, 2013.

_____. "Cultural Attitudes in Western Christianity Toward the Community of Goods in Acts 2 and 4." *Mennonite Quarterly Review* 78, no. 2 (April 1, 2004): 235-270. *ATLA Religion Database with ATLASerials*, EBSCO*host*. Accessed March 5, 2013.

Finn, Thomas M. *Early Christian Baptism and the Catechumenate: Italy, North Africa, and Egypt*. Collegeville, Minn: Liturgical Pr, 1992. *ATLA Religion Database with ATLASerials*, EBSCO*host*. Accessed March 6, 2013.

Flory, Richard W., and Donald E. Miller. "Expressive Communalism: The Embodied Spirituality of the Post-Boomer Generations." *Congregations* 30, no. 4 (September 1, 2004): 31-35. *ATLA Religion Database with ATLASerials*, EBSCO*host*. Accessed September 28, 2013.

Foulkes, Francis. "Review of God so Loved the Third World, by Thomas D. Hanks." *Themelios, No. 3, April 1984* 9 (1984).

Frend, William H. C. "Blandina and Perpetua: Two Early Christian Heroines" In *Women in Early Christianity*. Vol. XIV of Studies in Earlier Christianity, edited by David M. Scholer. New York, NY: Garland Publishing, Inc., 1993.

Guthrie, Shirley C., Jr. *Christian Doctrine*. Louisville, KY: Westminster/John Knox Press, 1994.

Gutierrez, Gustavo. *A Theology of Liberation*. rev. ed. Maryknoll, NY: Orbis Books, 1988.

Hackett, Conrad. "Emerging Adult Participation in Congregations." 2009. Accessed at September 28, 2013. http://www.changingsea.net/essays/Hackett.pdf.

Hahn, Scott W. *The Kingdom of God as Liturgical Empire: A Theological Commentary on 1-2 Chronicles*. Grand Rapids, MI: Baker Academic Press, 2012.

Halporn, James W. "Literary History and Generic Expectations in the Passio and Acta Perpetuae." *Vigiliae Christianae* 45, no. 3 (September 1, 1991): 223-241. *ATLA Religion Database with ATLASerials*, EBSCO*host*. Accessed March 6, 2013.

_____. *Passio Sanctarum: Perpetuae et Felicitatis*. Bryn Mawr Latin Commentaries, edited by Julia Haig Gaisser and James J. O'Donnell. Bryn Mawr, PA: Bryn Mawr College, 1984.

Hayes, Mike. *Googling God: The Religious Landscape of People in their 20s and 30s*. Mahwah, NJ: Paulist Press, 2007.

Heffernan, Thomas J. "Martyrdom, Charisma, and Imitation: Paths to Christian Sanctity." *Greek Orthodox Theological Review* 55, no. 1-4 (March 1, 2010): 251-267. *ATLA Religion Database with ATLASerials*, EBSCO*host*. Accessed March 6, 2013.

Hintz, August W. "The Pastor as Friend." Edited by Ralph G. Turnbull. *Baker's Dictionary of Practical Theology*. Grand Rapids, MI: Baker Book House, 1967.

Horrell, J. Scott. "Review of We Drink from Our Own Wells: The Spiritual Journey of a People, by Gustavo Gutierrez." *Themelios, No. 2, January 1986* 11 (1986).

Humphrey, B. Bruce. *Ministry on Fire: Fanning the Flame of Your Congregation.* St. Louis, MO: Chalice Press, 2005.

Icenogle, Gareth. *Biblical Foundations for Small Group Ministry.* Downers Grove, IL: InterVarsity Press, 1994.

Irvin, Dale T., and Scott W. Sunquist. *History of the World Christian Movement.* Maryknoll, NY: Orbis Books, 2001.

Japhet, Sara. *The Ideology of the Book of Chronicles and Its Place in Biblical Thought.* Translated by Anna Barber. Winona Lake, IN: Eisenbrauns, 2009.

Jarick, John. *2 Chronicles.* Sheffield, UK: Pheonix Press, 2007.

Johnson, Maxwell E. "Early Christian Baptism and the Catechumenate: Italy, North Africa, and Egypt." *Worship* 67, no. 2 (March 1, 1993): 182-184. *ATLA Religion Database with ATLASerials*, EBSCO*host.* Accessed March 6, 2013.

Johnstone, William. *2 Chronicles 10-36: Guilt and Atonement.* Vol. 2, *1 and 2 Chronicles.* Sheffield, UK: Sheffield Academic Press, 1998.

Jones, Beth Felker. "Emerging as Adults." *Christian Century* 129, no. 25 (December 12, 2012): 43-44. *ATLA Religion Database with ATLASerials*, EBSCO*host.* Accessed September 25, 2013.

Kater, John L, Jr. "Whatever Happened to Liberation Theology? New Directions for Theological Reflection in Latin America." *Anglican Theological Review* 83, no. 4 (September 1, 2001): 735-773. *ATLA Religion Database with ATLASerials*, EBSCO*host.* Accessed September 15, 2013.

Kiesling, Chris A. "A Long Adolescence in a Lame Direction? What Should We Make of the Changing Structure and Meaning of Young Adulthood?" *Christian Education Journal* 5, no. 1

(March 1, 2008): 11-27. *ATLA Religion Database with ATLASerials*, EBSCO*host*. Accessed September 27, 2013.

Klawiter, Frederick C. "The Role of Martyrdom and Persecution in Developing the Priestly Authority of Women in Early Christianity: A Case Study of Montanism." *Church History* 49, no. 3 (September 1, 1980): 251-261. *ATLA Religion Database with ATLASerials*, EBSCO*host*. Accessed March 6, 2013.

Landon, Michael. "The Social Presuppositions of Early Liberation Theology." *Restoration Quarterly* 47, no. 1 (January 1, 2005): 13-31. *ATLA Religion Database with ATLASerials*, EBSCO*host*. Accessed September 15, 2013.

Lefkowitz, Mary R. "Motivations for St Perpetua's Martyrdom." *Journal Of The American Academy Of Religion* 44, no. 3 (September 1, 1976): 417-421. *ATLA Religion Database with ATLASerials*, EBSCO*host*. Accessed March 6, 2013.

Long, Jimmy. *Emerging Hope: A Strategy for Reaching Postmodern Generations*, 2nd ed. Downers Grove, IL: InterVarsity Press, 2004.

Lose, David. *Confessing Jesus Christ: Preaching in a Postmodern World*. Grand Rapids, MI: Eerdmans, 2003.

MacKendrick, Paul. "From the Military Anarchy to the Arab Invasion" In *The North African Stones Speak*. Chapel Hill, NC: University of North Carolina Press, 1980.

Macquarrie, John. *Jesus Christ in Modern Thought*. 1990. Reprint. Harrisburg, PA: Trinity Press International, 1991.

Mahoney, Annette. "Marriage and Family, Faith, and Spirituality among Emerging Adults." 2010. Accessed at September 3, 2014. http://doc.wrlc.org/bitstream/handle/2041/122317/Mahoney_Marriage-Faith.pdf?sequence=1.

Markey, John J. "Praxis in Liberation Theology: Some Clarifications." *Missiology* 23, no. 2 (April 1, 1995): 179-195. *ATLA Religion Database with ATLASerials*, EBSCO*host*. Accessed September 15, 2013.

McCann, Dennis P. *Christian Realism and Liberation Theology: Practical Theologies in Creative Conflict*. Maryknoll, NY: Orbis Books, 1981.

McGowan, Andrew. "Discipline and Diet: Feeding the Martyrs in Roman Carthage." *Harvard Theological Review* 96, no. 4 (October 1, 2003): 455-476. *ATLA Religion Database with ATLASerials*, EBSCO*host*. Accessed March 6, 2013.

McGrath, Alister E. *Christian Theology: An Introduction.* 5th. West Sussex, UK: Wiley-Blackwell, 2011.

McIntosh, Gary L. *One Church, Four Generations: Understanding and Reaching All Ages in Your Church*. Grand Rapids, MI: Baker Books, 2002.

McKenzie, Steven L. *1-2 Chronicles. Abingdon Old Testament Commentaries*. Nashville, TN: Abingdon Press, 2004.

McManners, John. ed. *The Oxford History of Christianity*. New York, NY: Oxford University Press, 1990.

Merritt, Carol Howard. *Tribal Church: Ministering to the Missing Generation*. Herndon, VA: The Alban Institute, 2007.

Migliore, Daniel L. *Faith Seeking Understanding: An Introduction to Christian Theology*. 2nd. Grand Rapids, MI: Wm. B. Eerdmans Publishing Co., 2004.

Miller, Patricia Cox. "A Dubious Twilight: Reflections on Dreams in Patristic Literature." *Church History* 55, no. 2 (June 1, 1986): 153-164. *ATLA Religion Database with ATLASerials*, EBSCO*host*. Accessed March 6, 2013.

Mills, Watson E. ed. *Mercer Dictionary of the Bible*. Macon, GA: Mercer University Press, 1991.

Munoa, Phillip B, III. "Jesus, the Merkavah, and Martyrdom in early Christian Tradition." *Journal Of Biblical Literature* 121, no. 2 (June 1, 2002): 303-325. *ATLA Religion Database with ATLASerials*, EBSCO*host*. Accessed March 6, 2013.

Musser, Donald W., and Joseph L. Price. *New and Enlarged Handbook of Christian Theology*. Nashville, TN: Abingdon Press, 2003.

Nessan, Craig L. "Basic Christian Community: Liberation Theology in Praxis." *Currents In Theology And Mission* 15, no. 4 (August 1, 1988): 336-341. ATLA Religion Database with ATLASerials, EBSCOhost. Accessed September 15, 2013.

Oakley, Nigel W. "Base Ecclesial Communities and Community Ministry: Some Freirean Points of Comparison and Difference." *Political Theology* 5, no. 4 (October 1, 2004): 447-465. *ATLA Religion Database with ATLASerials*, EBSCO*host*. Accessed September 29, 2013.

O'Connor, June. "Process Theology and Liberation Theology: Theological and Ethical Reflections." *Horizons* 7, no. 2 (September 1, 1980): 231-247. *ATLA Religion Database with ATLASerials*, EBSCO*host*. Accessed September 15, 2013.

Parks, Sharon. *Big Questions, Worthy Dreams: Mentoring Young Adults in Their Search for Meaning, Purpose, and Faith*. San Francisco, CA: Jossey-Bass, 2000.

Pettersen, Alvyn. "Perpetua - Prisoner of Conscience." *Vigiliae Christianae* 41, no. 2 (June 1, 1987): 139-153. *ATLA Religion Database with ATLASerials*, EBSCO*host*. Accessed March 6, 2013.

Phelps, Jamie T. "Communion Ecclesiology and Black Liberation Theology." *Theological Studies* 61, no. 4 (December 1, 2000): 672-699. *ATLA Religion Database with ATLASerials*, EBSCO*host*. Accessed September 15, 2013.

Pizzolato, Luigi Franco. "Note Alla Passio Perpetuae et Felicitatis." *Vigiliae Christianae* 34, no. 2 (June 1, 1980): 105-119. *ATLA Religion Database with ATLASerials*, EBSCO*host*. Accessed March 6, 2013.

Polhill, John B. *Acts*, Vol. 26, *The New American Commentary*. Nashville, TN: Broadman and Holman Publishers, 1995.

Polhill, John. "Acts, Book Of" In *Holman Illustrated Bible Dictionary*, edited by Chad Brand, Charles Draper, Archie England et al. Nashville, TN: Holman Bible Publishers, 2003.

Powell, Mark Allan. "Acts of the Apostles" In *The HarperCollins Bible Dictionary*, edited by Mark Allan Powell, Third Edition. New York, NY: HarperCollins, 2011.

Rainer, Thom S., and Sam S. Rainer. *Essential Church? Reclaiming a Generation of Dropouts.* Nashville, TN: B and H, 2008.

Reid, Daniel G., Robert Dean Linder, Bruce L. Shelley, and Harry S. Stout. *Dictionary of Christianity in America*. Downers Grove, IL: InterVarsity Press, 1990.

Richard W. Flory and Donald E. Miller, eds., *GenX Religion*. New York, NY: Routledge, 2000.

Richardson, Rick. "Emerging Adults and the Future of Missions." *International Bulletin Of Missionary Research* 37, no. 2 (April 1, 2013): 79-84. *ATLA Religion Database with ATLASerials*, EBSCO*host*. Accessed September 25, 2013.

Rolheiser, Ronald. *The Holy Longing: The Search for a Christian Spirituality.* New York, NY: Doubleday, 1999.

Rosenbaum, Jonathan. "Hezekiah's Reform and the Deuteronomistic Tradition." *Harvard Theological Review* 72, no. 1-2 (January 1, 1979): 23-43. *ATLA Religion Database with ATLASerials*, EBSCO*host*. Accessed May 19, 2013.

Rutschman, LaVerne A. "Anabaptism and Liberation Theology." *Mennonite Quarterly Review* 55, no. 3 (July 1, 1981): 255-270. *ATLA Religion Database with ATLASerials*, EBSCO*host*. Accessed September 15, 2013.

⎯⎯⎯⎯. "Latin American Liberation Theology and Radical Anabaptism." *Journal Of Ecumenical Studies* 19, no. 1 (December 1, 1982): 38-56. *ATLA Religion Database with ATLASerials*, EBSCO*host*. Accessed September 15, 2013.

Salisbury, Joyce E. *Perpetua's Passion: The Death and Memory of a Young Roman Woman.* New York, NY: Routledge, 1997.

Scholer, David M. "And I was a Man: The Power and Problem of Perpetua." *Daughters Of Sarah* 15, no. 5 (September 1, 1989): 10-14. *ATLA Religion Database with ATLASerials*, EBSCO*host*. Accessed March 6, 2013.

Setran, David P., and Chris A. Kiesling. *Spiritual Formation in Emerging Adulthood: A Practical Theology for College and Young Adult Ministry.* Grand Rapids, MI: Baker Academic, 2013.

Smith, Christian, and Jane Thayer. "Inside Story of a Landmark Study on the Religious and Spiritual Lives of Emerging Adults: An Interview with Christian Smith." *Christian Education Journal* 8, no. 2 (September 1, 2011): 331-344. *ATLA Religion Database with ATLASerials*, EBSCO*host*. Accessed September 25, 2013.

Smith, Christian. *Lost in Transition: The Dark Side of Emerging Adulthood.* New York, NY: Oxford University Press, 2011.

Smith, Christian. *Souls in Transition: The Religious and Spiritual Lives of Emerging Adults.* New York, NY: Oxford University Press, 2009.

Smith, David L. *A Handbook of Contemporary Theology: Tracing Trends & Discerning Directions in Today's Theological Landscape.* Grand Rapids, MI: BridgePoint Books, 1998.

Stephens III, Benjamin, and Ralph C. Watkins. *From Jay-Z to Jesus: Reaching and Teaching Young Adults in the Black Church.* Valley Forge, PA: Judson Press, 2009.

Sterling, Gregory E. "Athletes of Virtue: An Analysis of the Summaries in Acts (2:41-47; 4:32-35; 5:12-16)." *Journal Of Biblical Literature* 113, no. 4 (December 1, 1994): 679-696. *ATLA Religion Database with ATLASerials*, EBSCO*host*. Accessed February 13, 2013.

Stewart-Sykes, Alistair. "Catechumenate and Contra-Culture: The Social Process of Catechumenate in Third-Century Africa and its Development." *St Vladimir's Theological Quarterly* 47, no. 3-4 (January 1, 2003): 289-306. *ATLA Religion Database with ATLASerials*, EBSCO*host*. Accessed March 6, 2013.

Streete, Gail P. C., *Redeemed Bodies: Women Martyrs in Early Christianity.* Louisville, KY: Westminster John Knox Press, 2009.

Sullivan, Lisa M. "I Responded, 'I Will Not...: Christianity as Catalyst for Resistance in the Passio Perpetuae et Felicitatis." *Semeia* no. 79 (January 1, 1997): 63-74. *ATLA Religion Database with ATLASerials*, EBSCO*host*. Accessed March 6, 2013.

Sundene, Jana L., and Richard R. Dunn. *Shaping the Journey of Emerging Adults: Life-Giving Rhythms for Spiritual Transformation.* Downers Grove, IL: InterVarsity Press, 2012.

Sutphin, Stanley T. *Options in Contemporary Theology*. Washington, DC: University Press of America, 1977.

Tabbernee, William. "Perpetua, Montanism, and Christian Ministry in Carthage c. 203 C.E." *Perspectives In Religious Studies* 32, no. 4 (December 1, 2005): 421-441. *ATLA Religion Database with ATLASerials*, EBSCO*host*. Accessed March 6, 2013.

Thoennes, Donna. "Keeping it Real: Research Findings on Authentic Community." *Christian Education Journal* 5, no. 1 (March 1, 2008): 76-87. *ATLA Religion Database with ATLASerials*, EBSCO*host*. Accessed September 29, 2013.

Thomas, Norman E. "Evangelism and Liberation Theology." *Missiology* 9, no. 4 (October 1, 1981): 473-484. *ATLA Religion Database with ATLASerials*, EBSCO*host*. Accessed September 15, 2013.

Tiede, David L. "Acts 2:1-47." *Interpretation 33*, no. 1 (January 1, 1979): 62-67. ATLA *Religion Database with ATLASerials,* EBSCO*host*. Accessed February 13, 2013.

Tilley, Maureen A. "Scripture as an Element of Social Control: Two Martyr Stories of Christian North Africa." *Harvard Theological Review* 83, no. 4 (October 1, 1990): 383-397. *ATLA Religion Database with ATLASerials*, EBSCO*host*. Accessed March 6, 2013.

Tracy, David. *Plurality and Ambiguity: Hermeneutics, Religion and Hope*. San Francisco, CA: Harper & Row, 1987.

van der Horst, Pieter W. "Hellenistic Parallels to the Acts of the Apostles 2:1-47." *Journal For The Study Of The New Testament* no. 25 (October 1, 1985): 49-60. *ATLA Religion Database with ATLASerials*, EBSCO*host*. Accessed February 13, 2013.

Volf, Miroslav. "Materiality of Salvation: An Investigation in the Soteriologies of Liberation and Pentecostal Theologies."

Journal Of Ecumenical Studies 26, no. 3 (June 1, 1989): 447-467. *ATLA Religion Database with ATLASerials*, EBSCO*host*. Accessed September 15, 2013.

Wall, Robert W. "The Acts of the Apostles" In *Acts; Introduction to Epistolary Literature; Romans; 1 Corinthians*. Vol. X of *The New Interpreter's Bible*. Nashville, TN: Abingdon Press, 2002.

Watkins, Ralph C. *The Gospel Remix: Reaching the Hip Hop Generation*. Valley Forge, PA: Judson Press, 2007.

Weaver, Rebecca H. "Wealth and Poverty in the Early Church." *Interpretation* 41, no. 4 (October 1, 1987): 368-381. *ATLA Religion Database with ATLASerials*, EBSCO*host*. Accessed March 6, 2013.

Welch, Adam C. *The Work of the Chronicler: Its Purpose and Its Date*. London, UK: Oxford University Press, 1939.

Williams, Demetrius K. "The Acts of the Apostles" In *True to Our Native Land: An African American New Testament Commentary*, edited by Brian K. Blount, 213-248. Minneapolis, MN: Fortress Press, 2007.

Wuthnow, Robert. *After the Baby Boomers: How Twenty - and Thirty - Somethings Are Shaping the Future of American Religion*. Princeton, NJ: Princeton University Press, 2007.

Wypustek, Andrzej. "Magic, Montanism, Perpetua, and the Severan Persecution." *Vigiliae Christianae* 51, no. 3 (August 1, 1997): 276-297. *ATLA Religion Database with ATLASerials*, EBSCO*host*. Accessed March 6, 2013.

www.ingramcontent.com/pod-product-compliance
Lightning Source LLC
Chambersburg PA
CBHW050633300426
44112CB00012B/1772